Beyond the Sale
–for Real Estate Agents–

How to Create a Great Business and a Life You Love

Discover the Secrets to Success, Including
Seven Keys from Top-Producing Agents

by Jerri Udelson & Ken Tutunjian

Tremont Press

Boston

Beyond the Sale—for Real Estate Agents—How to Create a Great Business and a Life You Love

Udelson, Jerri and Tutunjian, Ken, authors

Quantity discounts available. Contact info@tremontpress.com for information.

ISBN 978-0-692-07602-6

Cover design by Alex Hanna invisiblecitydesigns.com

Interior design by Katie Mingo

www.TremontPress.com

To Dad,
Who piqued my curiosity about all things business,

and

To Jeff,
For inspiring me with your creativity and supporting me with love.

—Jerri

To the many Realtors® who have worked with me, challenged me,
and enabled me to get better at my job.

—Ken

CONTENTS

Introduction   1

Part I
Creating a Great Business   7

1. What Do You Want to Create?   9
2. How to Create What You Want: Inner Actions   21
3. How to Create What You Want: Outer Actions   31
4. It's All About Connection   41
5. Designing Creative Marketing Strategies That Work   51
6. Putting It All Together: Designing and Implementing
    Your Business and Marketing Plan   65
7. Guiding Principles: Commitment, Accountability,
    and Legal and Ethical Standards   81

Part II
Creating a Life You Love   89

8. How to Create a Life You Love   91
9. (Optional) How to Create an Intimate Relationship   101

Part III
Tips from Top Producers:
Seven Keys to Success   109

Key **1**: Provide Extraordinary Service   111
Key **2**: Maximize Your Time   115
Key **3**: Set Boundaries   119
Key **4**: Become Great at Delegating   124
Key **5**: Take Great Care of Yourself   130
Key **6**: Give Back   136
Key **7**: Express Gratefulness   138

Conclusion   143

Blueprint for Success   149

Appendix **A**: Models for Operating a Successful Real Estate Business   173

Appendix **B**: List of Exercises   177

Resources   179

Acknowledgments   185

About the Authors   187

Introduction

This book is for:

- <u>The rainmaker</u>:
  You're the number one agent in your office. You manage a team of five. You're the go-to agent in your town. You haven't taken more than a day off in five months. And your blood pressure is elevated. You can't get off the real estate treadmill and onto the elliptical instead.

- <u>The struggling "not-so-newcomer"</u>:
  You've been in real estate for a few years. You have a number of transactions under your belt, but your business hasn't really taken off yet. You want to ramp it up and try different approaches, but you don't know where to start.

- <u>The experienced agent</u>:
  You make a ton of money, but still feel something is missing. You long to make a bigger contribution to your community, but haven't yet figured out how. And, there's a whole creative side of you that's unexpressed.

- <u>The recently transplanted agent</u>:
  You're an experienced agent new in town. You've created your website, passed out handfuls of business cards at your local Rotary Club meeting, done the same at your college reunion, sent out an email blast, and started a Facebook page for your business. Now you're waiting for the phone to ring, and not much is happening.

- The "lone ranger":
  You've been in business for five years. You've hit a plateau, and the techniques and strategies that used to work for you aren't anymore. It's time to become re-energized and inspired.

- The sales manager:
  You're an experienced manager and you want to support and grow your agents and staff. You want to learn a coach-like approach to developing your team.

Beyond the Sale: How to Create a Great Business and a Life You Love is based on our many years of combined experience working with real estate professionals. Jerri is a master business coach to top-producing and aspiring top-producing real estate agents and brokers and other professionals across the nation. Ken is the highly accomplished manager of two of the top residential brokerage offices in Boston, where he both trains and coaches many of the top agents in the city.

People come to us for coaching with a desire to achieve more success in their businesses <u>and</u> also to have happy and fulfilling lives. This book reflects our experience and perspectives as coaches and licensed real estate brokers working with agents and other professionals. **It is a distillation of practical principles, techniques and strategies <u>that actually work</u> to enable you to grow your business quickly and to create a life you love.**

This is not a "one size fits all" program.

Unlike many "brand name" sales trainers who call themselves coaches, we are not slick pitchmen, accustomed to standing in front of a large audience telling you how successful we are and how rich you will become if you would just follow our plan. In fact, we present no plan at all, no prescribed way of growing your business, and no "foolproof" marketing system (*e.g., make five cold calls, send three texts, write four hand-written cards a day...*). This is not a cookbook approach to fame and fortune.

Instead, we offer an <u>interactive process</u> where you are asked to look at your own strengths, your values, your interests, your past successes, and your business and life goals and then design a plan around these—a plan that you will be <u>eager</u> to implement and that will work <u>for you</u>. This is an <u>individualized</u> approach, much like the coaching process itself.

So what exactly is coaching?

Coaching has been described as *"a professional relationship that helps people produce extraordinary results in their lives, careers, businesses or organizations... Coaches partner with their clients to design the life they want (and to) bring out their clients' own brilliance and resources,"* according to Patrick Williams, founder of the Institute for Life Coach Training.

"(C)oaching is chiefly about discovery, awareness and choice. It is a way of effectively empowering people to find their own answers, encouraging and supporting them on the path as they continue to make important choices...A coach is someone who cares that people create what they say they want, that they follow through when they choose," write Whitworth, et. al, founders of The Coaches Training Institute.

Throughout the book we take a coach-like approach, asking thought-provoking questions that lead you to insights, to new ways of being and acting, and most importantly, to <u>powerful results</u>.

There are three "secret ingredients" in this book:

- Proven coaching techniques that incorporate long-time wisdom about creating results;
- Effective business- and life strategies derived from current research on topics such as time management, accountability, and self-care; and
- Practical tips for success gleaned from our work with a number of the nation's top producers.

By making use of these "secret ingredients" you will be able to reach your goals faster and easier than by using more conventional means.

A word about the approach....

Beyond the Sale was written for real estate agents <u>with some experience under their belts</u>. This is not an instruction manual. It is not a substitute for basic real estate sales training. You will not learn how to do a listing presentation or negotiate an offer. What you <u>will</u> learn, however, is how to create a vision for your business and for your life, how to create goals and action steps to help you move forward, how to design creative marketing strategies, and then – what to do after you have it all.

This is an exciting process of <u>self-discovery</u> and <u>strategic action</u> that can change your business and your life.

This book is designed to be interactive. As in a live coaching session with one of us, we ask you a lot of provocative questions that will help you gain valuable insights into the ways that you currently think and operate. As you ponder our questions, you will get new perspectives on your business and on your life. These new insights and perspectives will enable you to think differently and to act strategically, leading to powerful and profound results.

This book was written as a workbook, with many thought-provoking questions to answer and spaces for your ideas, insights and reflections. If you just read it like a novel, you won't get the best outcome.

We recommend that you <u>read the book completely first</u>, then go back and do the exercises in each chapter. If you skip over the questions and hurry along, you'll get about as much benefit as if you read an exercise book before going to bed and never went to the gym.

To ensure your success....

<u>Commit yourself to the process</u>.

- Approach this endeavor with integrity. As you know, integrity is the foundation of a successful business—and a successful life.

- Make time to read the material and complete the exercises.

- Answer the questions <u>as fully and as honestly</u> as you can.

You may find some of the questions challenging, but the more time and the more thought that you put into your answers, the more value you will receive in the end.

We realize that some of the exercises ask you to reflect on yourself in a way that may be unfamiliar to you. Please suspend judgment, and approach this book <u>with an open mind</u> and the <u>expectation of success</u>.

**Wherever you are right now is perfect—
it's your starting point, not your ending point.**

You might want to get together with an accountability partner as you work through the material. A partner (whether a team member, friend, manager or coach) will help you stay on track, support you, and make sure that you fulfill your commitments to yourself.

Finally, and, most importantly, to get the best results you need to <u>implement</u> the actions that you decide to take. Without action, even the best ideas will be of little use.

Before you begin....

You will get the most value from this book if you do three things before you begin:

1. Block out an hour or two at least once a week for the next four or five weeks <u>in your calendar</u> to read the book and complete the exercises. <u>Actually make an appointment with yourself</u> to do the reading and complete the exercises.

2. Go to www.gallupstrengthscenter.com and purchase the 1-34 Clifton Strengthsfinder ® assessment (i.e., "<u>all 34 strengths access</u>," which includes the Strengthsfinder 2.0 e-book). Take the computer assessment

to determine your <u>complete strengths</u> profile. The assessment takes less than 30 minutes to complete. Its use will be discussed in Chapter 3.

3. Gather data on your closed transactions for the past year or two. These data should include locations of properties, selling prices, commission information (commission rates, dollar amounts), and sources of business. You will be using this information later to assist you in developing a business and marketing plan.

And finally....

Ponder these questions:

* What would <u>a great business</u> look like to you?

* What would <u>a life you love</u> look like?

The answers to these questions will become crystal clear as you complete the exercises and move toward the goals that are most important to you.

Congratulations on taking these steps. You are about to begin an engaging and creative process.

PART 1

Creating a Great Business

CHAPTER 1

What Do You Want to Create?

As we begin to explore what you want to create in your business and in your personal life, it is important for you to get in touch with both your <u>values</u> and your <u>purpose</u>.

- <u>Values</u>: Your <u>values</u> are <u>the principles that are most important to you</u> in your life, what you most deeply care about. If you are living a life in harmony with your values, you will feel satisfaction and fulfillment. If you are living a life that does not honor and reflect your values, you will feel frustration and discord.

- <u>Purpose</u>: Your <u>purpose</u> is the <u>why</u>—the <u>reason</u> that you have chosen a particular way to express your values. It is what motivates, fuels, and energizes you, what gives you the drive to succeed. It is why you have chosen a career in real estate sales. Your purpose (i.e., your motivator) may change over time, as your needs and desires change. What drives you forward in your twenties might be very different from what drives you forward in your forties or fifties.

In this chapter you will identify your core values and your purpose. <u>You will also create five goals for your business</u>. In Chapters 2 and 3 you will learn how to make these goals a reality.

First, let's begin by identifying your values.

Your Values

"For me, I am driven by two main philosophies: know more today about the world than I knew yesterday and lessen the suffering of others. You'd be surprised how far that gets you."
– Neil deGrasse Tyson, author, astrophysicist and director of the Hayden Planetarium

"I had chosen to use my work as a reflection of my values."
–Sidney Poitier, actor (Guess Who's Coming to Dinner, Blackboard Jungle) and civil rights activist

"It's not hard to make decisions when you know what your values are."
– Roy E. Disney, former executive, Walt Disney Productions

Your values are the essence of who you are.

Values are your inner compass. They are qualities of life to which you are <u>naturally drawn</u>. When you are clear about your most important values, they can help guide you in creating a life of joy and meaning.

Values are not "shoulds," "oughts" or needs. If they are "good ideas," but they don't actually resonate with you on a deep level, then they are not values. If they have been with you since you were a child, then most likely they are values.

Jerri: As a young boy, Matt had a passion for designing and building things. He built and raced soapbox derby cars starting at the age of seven or eight. In college he majored in political science and minored in fine arts. After college Matt became an attorney and practiced law for many years. He always kept a woodshop at home and made sculptures and painted in his spare time. Now that he is retired, Matt spends many of his days designing landscapes, sculpting and woodworking. He says he is "happier than ever."

Expressing creativity is one of his highest values, and a source of great satisfaction and fulfillment.

Other examples of core values are:

To inspire	To lead	To create
To be loyal	To serve	To be healthy
To achieve	To love	To pursue knowledge
To take risks	To discover	To be challenged
To catalyze	To express beauty	To excel
To be wise	To contribute	To empower
To feel	To nurture	To be honest
To collaborate	To be powerful	To succeed
To innovate	To relate	To be recognized
To be connected	To educate	To be free

Exercise - What Are Your Top Three Values?

Using the examples in the paragraph above as a starting point, write down your top three values. Ask yourself, "What's most important to me?" You may want to look back to a time in your life when you were feeling most fulfilled and ask yourself which values were being expressed at that time.

1. Inspire

2. Love

3. Healthy

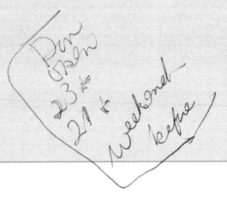

Your Purpose

"Everybody has a purpose. Your real job is to figure out why you're here and to get about the business of doing it."
– Oprah Winfrey

"Purpose is that feeling that you are a part of something bigger than yourself. That you are needed and that you have something better ahead to work for. Purpose is what creates true happiness."
– Mark Zuckerberg, Co-founder and CEO of Facebook

Your purpose is what motivates you, what keeps you going. It may change as you move through different stages of your life.

Discovering your purpose and staying connected to it will help you weather the ups and downs of this challenging profession. <u>Knowing why</u> you are doing the work you are doing will help you stay motivated, regardless of the circumstances.

Why are you in real estate? What need is it fulfilling in your life?

Jerri: Many of my clients have chosen a career in real estate because their top values are similar: achievement, independence, success, service, challenge, and creativity. Their purposes vary tremendously, however, from creating a business that will sustain their family and ensure a legacy for their children, to providing a vehicle for philanthropy in their community, to funding a lifestyle of travel and service abroad.

Ken: The agents in my office are in this business for a variety of reasons:

- Robert became an agent so that he could provide for his son and retire at age 50 with a certain amount of money in the bank. He is extremely motivated, and well on his way.

- Lila came from a very wealthy family. She had every advantage imaginable. Yet, she wanted to prove to herself that she wasn't just a "rich girl," that she could make it on her own. And through hard work and persistence she did.

- A number of years ago Alice was a social worker in an emergency room making $19,000 a year. She was tired of being underpaid and underappreciated. She wanted to use her "people skills" and professional training in an arena that would provide her more financial rewards and recognition. She decided to become a Realtor® and set a goal of making $120,000 a year. Within a few years Alice became adept at search engine optimization, and was able to use this technique to drive business to her website. And she was able to surpass her initial income goal.

Other agents want to prove to themselves that they have a "second act;" or leave a troubled marriage and start anew; or support a parent; or buy a second home and send their children to private schools; or use part of their earnings for philanthropy.

> **Ken:** It's never really about the money. If it's all about the money, it's never going to happen. If you're desperate, people can sense it and it drives them away.
>
> Your work must tie into your purpose. As Allan Dalton, former CEO of Realtor.com, used to say, "It's the biggest honor to be able to sell someone their home. It's where they laugh and where they cry. You get to earn your money doing that."

<u>What is your purpose</u> in choosing a career in real estate sales? What motivates you?

Exercise - What is Your Purpose?

Getting in touch with your purpose is important, as it will enable you to stay motivated and remain "in the game."

> **Ken:** The answer to this question won't be shared or graded, so be as forthright as possible. Dig deep inside and really be honest with yourself.

What is your purpose in being in real estate? What drives you?

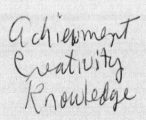

Achievement
Creativity
Knowledge

Where Are You Right Now?

Now that you've articulated your values and your purpose, it's time to ask yourself, "Where am I now? What's the current state of my business? What's the current state of my life?" It is important to see where you are <u>right now</u> before you begin to craft new goals for yourself and for your business.

As you look at what's working and what's not working, you will become clearer about what you want in your future. <u>What's working now that you can build upon? What's not working (or not working well enough) that you can change</u>?

**How close are you to where you want to be—
to your vision, to your ideal life?**

It's perfectly fine if there is a <u>large discrepancy</u> between <u>where you are right now</u> and <u>where you want to be</u>. It may feel uncomfortable, but it's actually the very tension inherent in this discrepancy (the "structural tension") that will propel you forward.

If you want to learn more about how structural tension is critical to the creative process, a good resource is *The Path of Least Resistance: Learning to Become the Creative Force in Your Own Life*, by Robert Fritz.

Exercise - Where Are You Right Now?

Think about your business for a moment. Think about what's working and what's not working for you. Then answer these questions <u>as honestly as you can</u>. These responses are important as you begin to reflect on what you want to create.

How much money did you make in the past 12 months?

$ _not much_

Are you on track right now to fulfilling your financial goals?

Yes _____ No ___✓___

Are you financially sound (e.g., paying your bills on time, being up-to-date on your mortgage, saving for the future)?

Yes ___✓___ No _____

Are you stressed about money?

Yes _____ No ___✓___

Do you have large credit card debt?

Yes _____ No ___✓___

Are you up-to-date on your taxes?

Yes ___✓___ No _____

Are you enjoying the way you are spending your time at work?

Yes ___✓___ No _____

Do you have a good working relationship with your manager?

Yes ___✓___ No _____

Do you have good relationships with the other agents and the staff in your office?

Yes ___✓___ No _____

How are you viewed by others in your office?

    As the go-to person? _____   As standoffish? _____

    Other? ___not in office to know___

Are you open to feedback from others? Yes ___✓___ No _____

Are you doing enough marketing? Yes ___✓___ No _____

Are you spending enough money on marketing?

Yes ___✓___ No _____

Do you have an effective system in place for prospecting?
Yes ___✓___ No _____

Do you have an effective system in place for following up on leads?
Yes ___✓___ No _____

Do you have an effective system in place for staying on track?
Yes ___✓___ No _____

Are you working with clients and customers you like?
Yes ___✓___ No _____

What type of clientele are you working with?

Eggheads with no motivation

What type of specialty, if any, do you have (e.g., short sales and foreclosures, first time buyers, empty nesters, seniors, luxury buyers)?

luxury, moveup, life changes

Are you involved in your community? Yes ___✓___ No _____

How would you rate your level of stress on a typical day?
(0 = no stress, 10= extreme stress) __✓__

What are the biggest stressors in your life? (circle)

Lack of money   Lack of personal time
~~Lack of sleep~~   Disorganization
Lack of support at home   Lack of support at work
Personal/relationship issues   Health issues
Fear   (Worry)
Other _need an office_
· plan that is quiet

How well are you sleeping at night? _____ no _____

Are you taking time off for yourself?
Yes _____ No _✓_____

Write any other thoughts that you have about your work life below:

lost soi -moved

Now go back and review the above answers. Which areas are of most concern to you?

lost soi

In which areas of your business do you want to make changes? Write your insights and ideas in the space below.

need a new soi close to home

Exercise - Creating Goals for Your Business

Now that you have thoroughly examined where you are, let's explore where you want to be.

Using your responses above as a guide, create five goals that you want to achieve for your business within the next twelve months. Write your goals in the present tense, in the positive (what you want—not what you don't want).

Here are several examples to get you started:

- *I have a new listing in the $x price range that is well-priced, with sellers who are easy to work with and who appreciate me.*

- *I am hiring the perfect buyer's agent by date.*

- *I am the go-to agent in the _____ neighborhood. I receive at least two referrals from past clients and customers every month.*

Notice how specific, unambiguous, and measurable the above goals are, and how they are written in the present tense.

In the space below, write five specific goals that you want to achieve for your business within the next twelve months. We suggest that one be a financial goal: *"I am making x dollars in the next twelve months."* **Make sure to choose goals that are results you truly want for yourself.**

1. I need 5 mkt able listings

2. Need 5 buyers

3. need a landing page

4. need how to max

5. how to come up at the search - top

Key Takeaways

- Your values are the principles that are most important to you. A fulfilling life is one lived in harmony with your values.

- Your purpose is what motivates you, what gives you the drive to succeed. It may change over time, as your needs change and your aspirations evolve.

- Before you can craft new goals for yourself, it is useful to see where you are right now. How close are you to your ideal life?

- In choosing goals for your business, make sure that they are specific, unambiguous, and measurable, and written in the present tense.

CHAPTER 2

How to Create What You Want:
Inner Actions

Everything we create in our lives is the result of both inner and outer actions. Inner actions are: what you tell yourself, what you believe about yourself, and how you visualize what you want. Outer actions are the steps that you take to bring what you want into reality. Both are important, but usually only outer actions are discussed in the domain of real estate.

It has been our experience, however, that so-called "inner actions" are as important in creating results as traditional action steps such as marketing, advertising and conducting open houses.

Let's look at inner actions first. These consist of

- Self-talk

- Self-belief

- Visualization (also known as mental imagery).

Self-Talk: What Are You Telling Yourself?

Self-talk is our internal dialogue, the thoughts and suggestions that we tell ourselves all day long. (*"I'm not prepared." "This is making me sick." "I'm not good enough." "I can't stand this." "I'm afraid of failing."*) These suggestions, albeit random thoughts and ideas that we may not even verbalize, are powerful, for they help create our reality.

As psychologist Shad Helmstetter, Ph.D. has written in *365 Days of Positive Self-Talk*, "*the thoughts you think and the words you say <u>physically</u> and <u>chemically</u> change your brain. Your self-talk literally wires your brain to succeed or fail.*"

What you tell yourself is key to creating results.

This is amazing

I love my work

I can do this

If you are fuzzy, ambiguous or negative, you will have difficulty manifesting what you want–or you will create negativity in your life, in your business, and in your personal relationships.

With self-talk you can either reinforce your intentions and move forward, or else undermine yourself and hold yourself back.

If you tell yourself "*I can never succeed in this business,*" or "*the market stinks,*" or "*the next quarter isn't going to be very good,*" or "*this job is killing me,*" how helpful are these thoughts in creating what you want?

That's why it is important to <u>state clear, powerful intentions</u>, such as "*I am the top-producing agent in my office,*" "*I love my work, and work with an incredibly dedicated, ethical and terrific team,*" and "*This year I am closing <u>x</u> transactions.*"

Other powerful statements are: "*This is amazing,*" "*I love this!*" "*This is engrossing,*" "*I feel such a sense of accomplishment,*" and "*I can do this!*"

These affirmations are extremely useful in helping you create what you want.

<u>Positive expectancy</u> (assuming the best) <u>coupled with powerful intentions</u> are two keys to creating the business and the life that you desire.

For the next week notice your thoughts. <u>Be honest with yourself</u>: **What are you telling yourself? Is your self-talk consistent with what you want to create?**

- If you notice yourself saying…

  "I'm never going to get this listing. I'm up against a more experienced agent."

- Say this instead…

  "I'm the perfect agent to represent this property. The seller will be fortunate to have me."

Exercise - What Are You Telling Yourself?

- In the space below, write down some of your negative self-talk that is not supporting you in having what you want.

- Then, create new intentions for yourself. Write these new intentions as positive affirmations, starting with *"I am…"* or *"I have…"* or *"This is…"* These new intentions are <u>powerful</u> suggestions that will help you create the results you desire.

- Finally, cross out each of the negative self-talk statements.

<u>Negative self-talk</u>	<u>New intentions</u>
1. ~~lost my~~ SOI	I have re invented my self
2. ~~do know not~~ know the market ~~here~~	Learned alot of the people & area

23

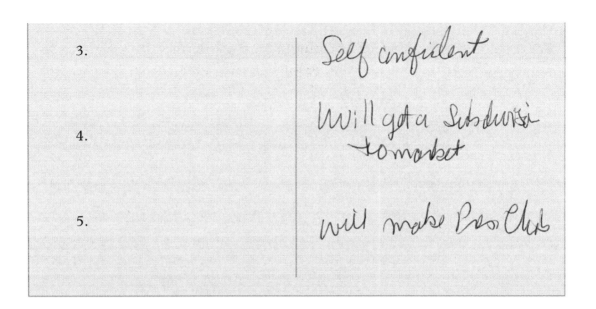

3.

4.

5.

Self confident

Will get a Subdivision
to market

will make Pres Club

What Do You Believe About Yourself?

"I am the greatest. I said that even before I knew I was."
– Muhammad Ali

Beliefs are extremely important in shaping your life.

Muhammad Ali, famed boxer and cultural icon, is an example of someone who had a tremendous belief in himself, starting at a young age. It was this brash self-confidence, coupled with talent and hard work, which enabled Ali to become a world champion.

<u>Positive belief in yourself</u> is another key to creating the life that you want. If you believe *"I can create whatever I want,"* or *"I'm great at attracting new clients,"* or *"I'm really talented,"* these beliefs will support you in having what you want.

If, on the other hand, you believe, *"I can never have _____,"* or *"I'm not worthy of a happy life,"* or *"I can't handle money,"* these negative, limiting beliefs can sabotage your success.

You might have grown up with negative beliefs; you might have learned them from your parents, your teachers, or your peers. These beliefs form part of the constant chatter in your head: *"I can't do this, this is too hard, I'm not good enough, this won't work out...."*

Once you realize that these beliefs aren't necessarily true, that they are old thought patterns as well as current habits of mind, you <u>can change your beliefs</u> to positive ones that support you.

<u>How do you create a new, positive belief?</u>

- Notice your negative, limiting belief.
- Ask yourself, "Does this belief support me in having what I want?"
- If not, create a new belief and imagine yourself embodying that belief. *How does it feel, for example, to be powerful, to be confident, to be creative?*

Exercise - What Do You Believe About Yourself?

- In the space below write three negative beliefs that you have about yourself.

<u>Negative Belief</u>	<u>New Belief</u>
1. not smart enough	Smarter than most people
2. Self doubt in my judgement	I know exactly what I am doing

3.

- Then change them to three new, positive beliefs, such as *"I am successful," "I am worthy,"* and *"I am powerful."*
- Imagine yourself embodying these new beliefs, and notice how you feel as you do so.
- Finally, cross out the negative beliefs.
- Post these new beliefs on an index card or on a sticky note on your bathroom mirror, your computer and other places where you will see them daily.

Visualizing What You Want

"If I can prepare myself the best way I can, that's all that matters."
– Michael Phelps, the most decorated Olympian of all time,
having won 28 medals, 23 of them gold

Phelps says he has been visualizing since he was 12 years old, watching what he calls his "videotape" of the perfect swim in his mind each night before going to sleep.

"He's the best I've ever seen and maybe the best ever in terms of visualization. He will see it exactly (as) the perfect race, and he will see it like he's...in the water."
– Bob Bowman, Phelps' longtime coach

Visualization (forming mental images) is a great technique that reinforces your goals by giving your subconscious mind distinct and detailed pictures of exactly what you want to achieve.

Visualization is as important in creating what you want as are self-talk and self-belief.

<u>To visualize:</u>

- Imagine a video of yourself accomplishing one or more of your goals. For example, imagine how you look as you receive an award from your company as top producer, or as you check your bank balance online and see that a large commission check has been deposited.

- Feel the emotions that accompany your achieving the goal. Are you feeling satisfied, elated, successful? Allow yourself to experience these feelings.

- You are sending a powerful suggestion to yourself that will enhance the manifestation process. The more detailed and "real" that you can make the visualization, the more effective it will be.

Other examples:

- Your goal is to be well-known in your community as a top Realtor®. In your visualization you imagine yourself opening the local newspaper and seeing a full page interview (with photos) featuring you and several of your clients. You feel happy, proud and accomplished as you read the article.

- You see yourself walking down the street when you run into a former client. She says, *"Wow, I see your signs everywhere. Congratulations!"* You are smiling; you feel satisfied and pleased by her comments.

Exercise - Visualizing Your Goals

In the space below, restate the goals that you have created on page 19.

1. 5 listings

2. 5 buyers

3. new subdivision

4. Pres Club

5. _____

Then, under each goal, write a brief description of what you are doing and how you are feeling as you accomplish that goal.

Now, sit in a quiet place and, if you want, close your eyes. In your mind, picture yourself having achieved each one of these goals.

<u>Do this exercise daily, in the morning and before bedtime for the next few weeks</u>. You may start noticing interesting "coincidences" and serendipitous events as you move closer to realizing your goals.

Write your observations in the space below.

Jerri: Many years ago I taught a course in setting goals, visualizing and developing intuition. It was remarkable how quickly and easily people achieved results using the above techniques. The mere act of writing down what you want to create and then visualizing it as accomplished is very powerful.

Optional Exercise: Creating a Vision Board

A vision board is a visual representation of your goals. It is a collage of pictures and phrases that embody your ideal life. Making one is a fun process that brings your goals to life.

To create a vision board:

- Gather a number of magazines.
- Cut out photographs, illustrations, words and phrases that represent your goals and your new beliefs.
- Glue the items to a large piece of cardboard.
- Hang the vision board in a place where you can see it several times a day.
- Update the pictures as your goals manifest and/or change.

For examples of completed vision boards, go to YouTube.com and search for "vision board examples" or Google "vision boards."

Key Takeaways

- Inner actions are important in creating results.
- They consist of:
    - Self-talk - what you tell yourself, your internal dialogue
    - Self-belief - what you believe about yourself
    - Visualization - the detailed mental pictures you create of your goals.
- You can change negative self-talk and self-beliefs to new, positive intentions and beliefs which will support you in having what you want.
- Visualization is a great way to reinforce what you want. Creating a vision board can help bring your goals to life.

CHAPTER 3

How to Create What You Want: Outer Actions

Playing to Your Strengths

Visualization, positive self-talk, and positive self-belief are vital to creating the business—and the life—that you want. Equally important is <u>taking action steps</u> that are effective, timely, direct and focused.

As a real estate professional you've been bombarded with trainings, webinars, blogs, and so forth telling you the best way to conduct your business. Do you farm a territory, make cold calls, pay for web referrals? The possibilities are endless.

There is no "one way" or "best way" to get buyers and listings, nor is there "one way" or "best way" to market yourself. What works for agent x may not work for you. <u>Which actions are best for you to take</u>? The answer is not very complicated:

Do what works for you, playing to your strengths.

By now, we hope that you taken the Clifton *StrengthsFinder* ® computer assessment (from gallupstrengthscenter.com as discussed in the Introduction) and determined your strengths profile. The StrengthsFinder assessment enables you to identify your own innate strengths—those talents that come most naturally to you.

According to author Tom Rath, there are 34 "themes" of talent, such as "Achiever®," "Command®," "Learner®," and "Woo®" (meaning winning others over). If you focus on your talents, on what you do best, you will be happier and more engrossed at work than if you focus instead on improving your weaknesses.

We often suggest that agents take the *Strengthsfinder 2.0 assessment* so that we can review the results together and see how they can leverage their top strengths in their work. We suggest that you do the same. It will be very revealing and helpful.

Exercise - Your Top Ten Strengths

In the space below, list your top ten strengths from the *StrengthsFinder 2.0* assessment. Include a brief description of each strength (*e.g., Activator® - turning thoughts into action*).

1.

2.

3.

4.

5.

6.

7.

8.

9.

10.

Then answer these questions in the spaces below:

<u>What impact did discovering your top ten strengths have on you?</u>

<u>How will you use this information as you move forward in your business?</u>

An important aside: Real estate is really a business about **relationships**; it's not about the deal. It's not about land values, mortgage rates, condominium by-laws, or prices per square foot. **It's about people.** <u>You need to establish the relationship before you can close the deal</u>.

The most successful agents we know have grown their businesses by <u>routinely</u> picking up the phone and speaking with past and potential clients, customers and referral sources. They also meet face-to-face with people. Some socialize with their clientele. Many have become leaders in their communities. Most are <u>consultants</u> and <u>trusted advisors</u> to their clients rather than <u>sales agents</u>.

If the thought of growing your business by <u>developing relationships</u> makes you uneasy or uncomfortable, it would be useful at this point to look inside yourself and see if this is really the right profession for you. If none of your top ten strengths involves working with others (if, for example, all ten of your strengths are "Learner®," "Deliberative®," "Context®," "Input®," "Adaptability®," "Futuristic®," "Discipline®," "Ideation®," "Consistency®," and "Intellection®") you might be happier in a profession based around <u>ideas</u> and <u>knowledge</u> rather than around <u>people</u>.

If your top strengths include talents such as "Woo®," "Command®," "Achiever®," "Activator®," "Empathy®," "Connectedness®," "Positivity®," and "Responsibility®," then you are most likely in the right profession and have many of the qualities of top producers.

Looking at and Building on Your Past Successes

Now that you've determined your innate strengths, it's time to take a different tack and look back and see what's worked for you in the past to build your business. You need to know your numbers and other important data both to understand how you got to be where you are right now, and to help you achieve your goals in the future.

> **Ken:** You have to know your business cold—where your buyers come from, where your listings come from. Knowing the source of your business is the foundation of growing it to where you want it to be.

<u>This information is key to creating a business and marketing plan</u>. After you have examined what's worked, you can repeat those actions. More importantly, as you see what hasn't worked, you can take different steps to ensure a better outcome. You might remember, as Albert Einstein supposedly said, *"Insanity: doing the same thing over and over again and expecting different results."*

Exercise - Looking at What's Worked for You

Take some time and gather data on your closed transactions from the past year or two. <u>Specifically, study your list of closed transactions</u>. Then answer the questions below as completely as you can:

How many transactions did you close in a year? _____

What was the average selling price of a property? $ _800,000_

What was the average commission (in dollars) $ _20K_

What was the average commission rate (percentage)? __5__ %

What percent of transactions were your own listings? __50__ %

What percent were from your buyers? __50__ %

Where were your transactions located (what cities or towns, which neighborhoods or areas?

_____

_____

Where did your business come from?

Note: If you have not been keeping a written record of the sources of your business (i.e., of <u>every</u> transaction) it is <u>critical</u> that you begin to do so now. *This is <u>extremely vital</u> information. It will enable you to evaluate your advertising efforts and marketing strategies and then take appropriate actions to build on what's working and to change what isn't.*

How many transactions came from <u>referrals</u> from your <u>sphere of influence</u>? __2__

(As a reminder, your sphere of influence or <u>SOI</u> is your database of people—family, friends, current and former clients and customers, other real estate professionals and business associates—who have done business with you, are doing business with you, may do business with you, or who refer business to you. The names are often categorized A, B, and C, depending upon the amount of business each person has done with you, your relationship with him or her, and other criteria of your choosing.)

Specifically, how many referrals were

From family? _____

From friends? _____

From neighbors? _____

From former clients and customers? _____

From mortgage brokers? _____

From attorneys? _____

From other agents? _____

From corporate referrals? _____

Relocation companies? _____

Other? _____

How many closed transactions came <u>from other sources</u> (non-referrals)?

From your website? _____

From social media? _____

From open houses? _____

From signs on properties? _____

From direct mailings? _____

From calls to FSBOs? _____

From calls to expired listing owners? _____

From sources not listed above *(for example, clubs to which you belong, your college alumni association, your gym, your children's schools)*? _____

Highlight or circle the top five sources of business.

Is there a common thread to your buyers and sellers? Do you have a particular niche? (For example: Are they in high-tech? Are they from a particular demographic? Are they international?) Write your answers below.

_____

_____

This is extremely valuable information. If you find that you are getting business from a particular source, it would be strategic to put more attention on cultivating this source.

Focus on expanding your business in areas where you have already been successful.

On the other hand, if you don't actually get business from certain activities that you have been doing for quite a while (such as running print ads in specific publications or attending early morning meetings with your leads group), either do the activity in a different way or discontinue it and try something new.

Exercise - Where Does Your Business Come From?

In the space below, answer these questions:

Which specific actions or strategies are generating most of your business (e.g., working with a certain buyer niche, making calls to your sphere of influence, posting on Facebook)?

1. Friends
2. Family
3. Friends of friends
4. FB
5. Garden Club / Gun Club

Who or what are the top three sources of referrals for your business?

1. Friends
2. Passed Clients
3. Clubs / organ.

> Which activities are generating the least amount of business and are draining your time and/or financial resources?
>
> 1. mailings
> 2. O.H
> 3. Desk Duty

All of your answers above are <u>critical</u>, as they tell you what's working and what to build upon. You can then expand upon this foundation with <u>new</u> strategies and activities to grow your business.

Key Takeaways

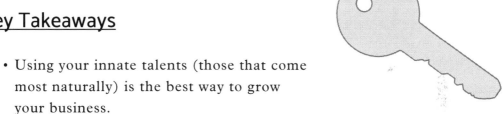

- Using your innate talents (those that come most naturally) is the best way to grow your business.

- Building on what's worked in the past is also a key to business success.

- Keeping track of the sources of your business will enable you to evaluate your sales, advertising and marketing efforts.

CHAPTER 4

It's All About Connection

> **"The business of business is relationships; the business of life is human connection."**
> – Robin Sharma, Canadian author and speaker

There are two facts about selling real estate that should be carved in stone:

1. Real estate is generally local. It is not that difficult to become well known—even famous—in your area as the go-to agent to buy and sell properties in your building, your block, your neighborhood, and even your city, town or suburb if you use the right strategies, systems and techniques.

2. The business of real estate is based upon relationships. People want to do business with people they like and trust. No matter how gorgeous your website may be, and how fascinating your tweets are, **you still need to get out and meet face-to-face with clients and customers.** You generally cannot sell a property to anonymous buyers over the internet the same way you can sell a vintage radio on eBay.

These facts make it fairly easy to market yourself in a relatively small, well-defined area, using techniques to enable you to become well known. The goal of a successful agent is to be <u>the person</u> who is engaged for real estate purchases and sales in his or her sphere of influence, neighborhood, and/or community.

Surprisingly, when we've met with a number of agents during coaching sessions in the past, more than a few were what we call "secret agents." Yes, they were real estate agents, but they hadn't told very many people about their profession, and thus had missed a number of opportunities to obtain new clients, customers and referrals.

Ken: An agent in my office was on the regional board of her college alumni association. The man sitting next to her at monthly board meetings for the past four years had turned to her and said, *"I won't be here next month. You won't be seeing much of me as I'm selling my house and moving out of town."*

The next day the agent stormed into my office, her hands flailing above her head in frustration and said, *"Can you believe this guy, not giving me the opportunity to list his house?"*

I asked her, *"Did you ever tell him you were in real estate?"*

She looked at me with daggers in her eyes, turned around and went back to her desk.

Don't be a secret agent!

This doesn't mean that you ought to be passing out business cards at wedding receptions and funerals. It does mean that you should tell people in your book club, volunteer organization and dog walking group that you are a Realtor®, and say it with pride and conviction.

- <u>Margot Rose Edde</u> is a broker associate at a medium-sized boutique firm in San Francisco. Margot left a lucrative career at a Back Bay, Boston agency to move to San Francisco and *"figure out what I was going to do next."* She left an area where she had a large number of family, friends and business connections and moved to a city where she knew no one except her brother.

"My life had become too much about real estate. I was always think[ing] friends could become clients and which clients might become friends."

On the West Coast she began teaching Pilates and yoga and did [some] consulting with start-ups. She also met her husband, an engineer and na[tive] San Franciscan. *"But I missed making money and introducing myself as a brok[er]. I have always taken immense pride in what I do. Helping clients find their home is a truly noble thing. So I decided to change the way I approached my career: I would approach work as an important piece of my life, not my entire life.*

"I wanted people to work with me because I had other facets to my life. I loved yoga and hiking. I knew I could be a top broker and also have a marriage, a family, and side interests.

"I decided to leverage my contacts in my natural networks in fitness and tech and in my growing social circles. I continued to teach exercise classes. At the end of each class I'd say, 'By the way, I just do this for fun. I'm really a real estate broker.'

"My husband carries my business cards and always tells people, 'My wife just sold...' He's not a natural salesperson, but he does it to support my business. And I go places where I meet people who share my interests. My attitude is: After talking to me, people need to feel that if they don't get my card, they are missing out on expert, insider advice. Now, most of my business is referral-based."

Lead Generation and Follow Up in a Connected World

Ken: Some of my agents are having a love affair with the postage meter. Instead of going out and prospecting for potential clients, customers and referral sources, they rely on sending out marketing pieces to generate business. Mailings are good, but they are a passive way of connecting with people. In my experience, sending out direct mailings is one of the least effective ways of getting clients and customers.

ore important than reaching for the phone and <u>actually</u>
a telephone conversation can deepen the relationship
on nuances often lost in emailing or texting. Voice-to-
prevent misunderstandings.

ot was a wonderful two-family Victorian property in
ad just started in real estate, and my manager showed
mber directory and told me to call FBSOs and speak to
called a number and asked for "Mr. Stein." I think he was so
used that I knew his name (unlike the other agents who had been calling him)
that he set up an appointment with me and gave me the listing.

There are now much better, easier, and faster ways to generate leads. Five systems, Vulcan 7, Mojo Dialer, ArchAgent PowerDialer, The RedX, and Espresso Agent are worth exploring.

- <u>Vulcan 7</u> is a lead generation system that provides phone numbers for FSBOs and probate leads and email addresses and phone numbers for expired listings. It can perform customized neighborhood searches (even searching for renters by area) and has an email feature.

- <u>Mojo Dialer</u> is an all-in-one "power dialing" prospecting system that can make as many as 300 calls per hour (using three phone lines) and manage leads, contacts and clients.

- <u>ArchAgent PowerDialer</u> is a web-based automatic dialing service that can be set up to preload your call lists. It will automatically transfer notes taken during the conversation to your customer relationship manager (CRM) or to your database. ArchAgent also offers lead management services.

- <u>TheRedX</u> is a lead generation, management and prospecting system for expired, FSBO and pre-foreclosure leads. It has an auto-dialer feature ("Storm Dialer") that can make up to 100 calls an hour and leave pre-recorded voice messages "with a single click."

- <u>EspressoAgent</u> delivers expired and FSBO leads to your power dialer daily. It also offers a CRM and lead management system

You can find out more about these systems on their websites or on

How do you follow up with <u>incoming leads</u> on a timely basis? There are <u>lead conversion</u> services of interest, especially if you have an internation clientele and need fast response times 24/7.

- <u>GetRileyNow.com</u> is a "custom concierge" service that responds to email leads within two to five minutes with a real person who follows your scripts. It's available 24/7. The service is $199, $299 or $499 a month, depending upon the number of leads.

- <u>Rokrbox.com</u> is a "lead conversion process" with "consistent and personalized follow up" that answers queries with a live person (available 80 hours per week) who can make appointments for consultations. Rokrbox also provides a "comprehensive prospecting system" for the BoomTown technology platform discussed later in this chapter. The cost ranges from $2000 to $3500 a month.

While the systems and services discussed above were state-of-the-art at presstime, we realize that technology is constantly evolving, and that what is hot today may be passé tomorrow. We have created a Facebook group, <u>Beyond the Sale—for Estate Agents</u>, which is an ongoing forum for you to ask and answer questions on topics including real estate technologies, techniques and systems. It is also a place for you to get support from us and from other agents throughout the country. <u>Take a moment and join now.</u>

Mastering Your Conversations: A Few Words About Scripts

Scripts are a time- and audience-tested way to keep you on track and to help you ask the right questions when you are speaking with prospective customers and clients, negotiating a commission, or asking for a referral.

>ts to agents, they often say, *"I'm not a bot, a telemarketer, rs."* But scripts are nothing more than a <u>map</u>. They are a e you have rehearsed a script, you can put it into your own d with your own inflections, and it will just come naturally.

ses scripts: Everyone on television uses scripts. So do cians use written scores. Some stick to the letter of the they all use a basic script.

You may hesitate to use something "canned," but if you <u>practice</u> relevant scripts, putting them <u>into your own words</u> and making them your own, you will have mastered key portions of the sales process.

If you are an agent with Coldwell Banker Residential Brokerage in New England, there is a publication called *Words That Work: Real World "Street Tested" Conversations and Dialogues for Today's Real Estate Professional* that contains a myriad of useful scripts. If you are not affiliated with CBRB, you can find several books on scripts at major booksellers. You can also find free scripts at www.mikeferry.com/main/content/complimentary. There are also a number of videos on YouTube that teach you how to use scripts. This might be more enjoyable than reading a text.

Let's Talk About Fear

Ken: I don't know anyone who goes from 0 to 100 in cold calls without fear and trepidation at the very beginning. Fear can be anything from fear of failure to fear of success to fear of rejection.

Jerri: If you are afraid of taking the steps that you know will help yo⟍ your business, you might want to ask yourself, *"What exactly am I afraid of?"*

It's okay to be afraid, it's even natural. How you <u>respond</u> to fear is the real issue. Fear can paralyze you. It can also energize you. And facing your fears head-on will expand your comfort zone and enable you to take on even greater challenges in the future.

As author and life coach Cheryl Richardson has written in *Stand Up for Your Life*, *"When we use fear to our advantage by tackling those things that evoke a sense of excitement and trepidation, fear becomes an ally…*

"Fear can challenge you, motivate you, and energize you to act…When you make friends with fear and step outside of your comfort zone, this zone expands. Then things that used to frighten you or seemed impossible become easier.

"Facing fear builds confidence and emotional strength… Anything worth doing in life will involve fear—whether it's talking to a stranger, giving a speech, or leaving a relationship that you know is holding you back."

Jerri: There's a book I recommend to clients by psychologist Susan Jeffers: *Feel the Fear and Do It Anyway*. It includes a ten-step program for dealing with negative self-talk. I often say, *"Just buy the book and look at the title everyday. You don't even need to read it!"* Facing your fears directly, either with the support of your manager, coach or a therapist, can be the most effective way of moving forward in any area of your business or your life that you've been avoiding.

It is also important to create new intentions for yourself—as discussed above—such as *"I am courageous," "I enjoy meeting new people,"* or *"I can handle any situation with grace and ease."*

The point being: Take inner action (work with powerful intentions and allow yourself to feel your emotions) followed by outer action (face your fears and take the steps you know you need to take).

Ken: It's normal to feel fearful. You just can't let fear stop you from moving forward. Take action. It's the only way you are going to learn. And practicing over and over will improve your skills and reduce your fear.

Ask yourself: *"How long do I want to sit with the fear before taking action?"* Then, take a deep breath and <u>just do it</u>!

Exercise - Looking at Fear

Remember a time when you were fearful. Choose a recent experience, if you can. What were you afraid of? (e.g., you were afraid to follow up with a client or you were afraid to ask for a referral.)

What did you tell yourself at the time? (For example, *"I'm afraid to call x because he won't extend his listing." "I can't do this."*)

How did you overcome your fear? (e.g., *"I took a deep breath and made the call."* Or: *"I procrastinated until the decision was made for me."*)

What could you have said and done instead? (For example, *"I told myself, 'I've got this! Let's <u>do</u> it!'" "I found a role-playing partner and role-played the situation with her. Then I went ahead and made the call."*)

How will you handle a similar situation in the future?

Key Takeaways

- Real estate is based upon relationships. You need to be engaged with people in your community. Then you will become well known.

- A number of technologies are available to assist you in lead generation and follow up.

- Scripts are a useful way to master specific conversations.

- Fear is a normal reaction to new, challenging situations. How you respond to fear is the issue, not the fear itself.

CHAPTER 5

Designing Creative Marketing Strategies That Work

In this chapter we discuss a number of ideas for creative marketing strategies that have worked for our clients. These include

- ways to expand your sphere of influence

- ways to stay connected to past buyers and sellers

- ways to ask directly for referrals

- ways to cultivate new referral sources

- ways to use social media to market your business

- ways to keep your website and social media timely, and

- ways to develop and protect your brand.

You can choose the ones that you want to implement as well as design ones of your own. In Chapter 6 you will put all of your work together and design a business and marketing plan that will work for you.

> **AS YOU ARE READING, CHECK OFF OR HIGHLIGHT THE IDEAS THAT HAVE THE MOST APPEAL TO YOU.**

Expanding Your Sphere of Influence

Ken: I tell my agents, *"Don't sit around thinking about getting new business. Step away from your desk. Get engaged. Go out into the real world and <u>do something</u>. Meet people."*

- Take a leadership position on the board of directors of a nonprofit organization that you want to support and that is worthy of your time and commitment.

- Sponsor a Little League baseball or youth soccer team.

- Take a lifelong learning class on a subject you are interested in, perhaps art appreciation or financial planning.

- Join a meetup group of people who share one of your interests. Topics range from hiking, dining, foreign film and backgammon to murder mysteries, sci-fi literature and new technology. You can find meetups in your area or start your own group at www.meetup.com.

- Co-sponsor a community program such as a free document shredding day or a "fingerprinting for kids" event with your local police department.

- Buy a table at a charity event, host some of your top clients, and purchase advertising in the program.

Ken: All of the social media in the world can't replace live interactions. A group of four newer agents in my office held a combination Sunday brunch/buyers seminar at a local restaurant. The room was packed with many of their friends. Lots of networking took place, and the agents made a number of business appointments as a result.

Staying Connected to Past Buyers and Sellers

- First and foremost, keep your list of contacts up-to-date in your contact management system. Remember to include email and street addresses, phone numbers, property closing dates, and birthday and anniversary dates for future use.

- Create a client and customer contact program.

  Examples:

  - Make time <u>each day</u> to call or meet with former clients, customers and referral sources to generate business. This could be something as simple as making calls to five former clients every morning. **These actions, done consistently, can produce powerful results.**

  - Send a handwritten note to buyers on the anniversary of their property closing.

Ken: The power of a handwritten note (as opposed to an email) is immense in this day and age. It shows extraordinary thoughtfulness and consideration.

- Send a monthly or quarterly email newsletter with market updates, information on local events and attractions, restaurant listings or reviews, and new community resources. *(Note: There are "canned" newsletters available for purchase. These often include recipes, articles on decorating your cottage or mountain retreat and so forth. We don't recommend purchasing these, as they do not showcase your expertise, and may not be relevant to your clientele.)*

- Call or text customers after a closing and then stop by with a bottle of wine or a gift basket and a handwritten note. (This would be in addition to sending a closing gift.)

- Institute a biweekly or monthly lunch or dinner where you take a client or customer out to say "thank you for your business" and to stay connected.

- Host a small event for clients who live in the same neighborhood to meet one another.

- Host a major event for all of your clients, customers and referral partners. The event could be as elaborate as renting out a museum and holding a cocktail party or as casual as hosting a summer barbeque.

Referrals: Ask for the Business

Ken: You have to ask for referrals directly. You cannot assume that people will automatically refer business to you. This is not a place where you can be a secret agent.

- On the bottom of any thank you notes or email blasts include text such as:

"I appreciate your referrals."

<u>Or</u>, *"Our business thrives on referrals from people who have had a great experience with us. If you feel we have met or exceeded your expectations, we would appreciate your passing our name along to others."*

<u>Or</u>, *"Please let me know if you have friends, family, associates or neighbors who could use an expert real estate professional to help them when buying or selling."*

<u>Or</u>, *"My business is referral-based. A referral from you to a friend or colleague is the best compliment I can receive."*

- Hold an event for clients and customers and others *"to thank you for your friendship, continued business and referrals."*

- Establish reciprocal referral arrangements with agents in other states, cities, towns, or neighborhoods into which or from which your clients might be moving (e.g., urban to suburban or one large city to another). Referrals are a great way to help clients outside of your local area, and referral fees can be a significant source of income.

- Get to know professionals who would be in a position to refer business to you. These include mortgage brokers, wealth managers, accountants, financial planners, geriatric case managers, and trusts & estates and real estate attorneys. Invite them to lunch or for coffee and let them know about your business. Ask them for a profile of their ideal clients so you can refer business to them as well.

- Send cards or small gifts for holidays and as thanks to your top referral sources.

  - Go through your database and mark the names of people who have sent you the most referrals in the past several years.

  - Make a separate list or spreadsheet of these top referral sources. Include all of their contact information and other relevant data on the list.

  - Create a program for contacting these people <u>at least quarterly</u> and sending handwritten notes and thank you gifts.

An important note: It may or may not be legal or ethical for you to take referral partners to lunch or to send them thank you gifts. In Chapter 7, Guiding Principles: Legal and Ethical Standards, we discuss this issue and suggest that you contact your attorney or real estate board for clarification, as the laws vary by state. It is, however, always appropriate to send handwritten thank you notes and to make phone calls to express your appreciation for referrals.

Using Social Media

Marketing by means of social media has become critical for agents, especially in the last ten years. Before the internet—and especially before Facebook (FB) and Instagram—agents could run ads in their local papers, pay for inserts in coupon mailers, give out refrigerator magnets, and attend networking events and feel that they had done a great job of marketing themselves and their listings. Many of these approaches are now outdated, given the ubiquity of the internet and the importance of social media.

Social media is vital for building your presence, expanding your network, engaging authentically with your audience, generating leads, promoting your brand, and driving traffic to your website.

It is a great way to showcase your expertise, to feature listings, and to promote open houses.

Right now Facebook and Instagram are the best online sources of leads, and therefore the first platforms to master as you grow your presence on social media. Both are social networking sites. Facebook is the world's largest online social media site. More than two billion people worldwide use Facebook every month. Users can post text, pictures and videos, and can comment on one another's posts. FB has a large number of features, including messaging and status update. You can set up special interest group pages, pay for ads and also pay to "boost" your posts.

Instagram (owned by Facebook) is an online photo- and video-sharing site. According to FB, *"one of every five minutes (that) people in the U.S. spend on mobile (technology) is on Facebook or Instagram."*

If you are just getting up to speed on social media, we recommend that you start with these two platforms and begin posting regularly. Comment on other people's posts and post articles that are timely and relevant to your target audience (such as community news and events and other local lifestyle information), rather than using posts solely to advertise yourself and your business.

"It is less important to always be on and more important to always be relevant," says Kyle Elizabeth, social media branding expert.

There are a number of good sources of articles that you can repost. Among the best are *The New York Times*, *The Washington Post*, *The Wall Street Journal*, Inman.com (real estate news for Realtors® and brokers), and Dwell.com. Reposting articles, commenting on them, and creating a dialogue with your readers will highlight your expertise and strengthen your online presence.

Be careful of alienating clients by posting political rants. If you really want to post about politics or social issues, it is better to repost an article from *The New York Times* or *The Wall Street Journal* and let the article speak for you.

"Social media is much more than posting photos of listings or links to articles," says Katie Lance, social media consultant and author of *#GetSocialSmart: How to Hone Your Social Media Strategy*. *"Real estate professionals need to create a content plan to get the most out of social media. When you create a video, a blog, or even a podcast, you are telling the story of what it feels like to work with you. Lean into who you are, and create content with your voice and your opinions. Consistency counts. Developing a consistent publishing schedule is key. It's also one of the best ways to drive traffic and leads to your social media platforms."*

It is important to create a Facebook page for your business that is separate and distinct from your personal timeline page. There are several reasons for this:

- Under Facebook's Terms of Service (TOS), you cannot use your personal timeline (personal FB page) *"primarily for your own commercial gain."* You need to use a business FB page for such purposes. If you violate the TOS, your account can be suspended.

- You cannot have more than one personal timeline, but you can have multiple business FB pages and FB special interest groups. And, of course, you can advertise on business FB pages and pay to boost your posts.

- It is much more professional to have a business page that features real estate and doesn't include pictures of your daughter's newest kitten or your vacation photos. Having one or more distinct Facebook pages for your business will reinforce the boundary between your business and your personal life.

One of the best features of Facebook for real estate professionals is that you can run highly targeted ads to a defined audience based on factors such as their demographics, locations, income levels and special interests. You can determine a daily budget, schedule ads, and pay to boost your posts to promote your page. Using FB to target home buyers and to drive visitors to your open houses can be a very effective way to market your business.

Facebook and Instagram videos are important marketing tools.

Videos provide an immediacy and foster engagement in a way that is difficult with just words and photographs. Make sure your videos are short, well-edited, and appealing.

Jill Boudreau, an agent in an upscale Boston suburb, uses very short videos to feature listings and to showcase her expertise in her market. She posts videos ranging from 30-second quarterly market reports to "Four Reasons to Stay in Town During Spring Break" to brief property tours. Her videos are well-shot, with fast-paced music and beautiful photography.

Once you have begun posting regularly on Facebook and Instagram, expand your social media presence to other platforms, including LinkedIn, YouTube, and Snapchat.

- LinkedIn is a great medium for growing your referral network. You can connect with people in specific industries (such as wealth managers and trusts & estates attorneys) and also sponsor content that is targeted to a specific audience.

- <u>YouTube</u> is a video-sharing site that lets you create and post videos. You can promote listings with video tours as well as share your expertise on real estate- and community-related topics.

- <u>Snapchat</u> is a popular app for millennials. Snapchat users can send very short videos that disappear after ten seconds of viewing. You can send photos with drawings, text and emojis that disappear after one to ten seconds. According to Omnicore, a digital marketing agency, seventy-one percent of users are under the age of 34, forty-five percent are between 18 and 24 years old, and seventy percent are female, making this an effective platform for advertising fast food, cosmetics, teen films, and so on.

Increasingly, Snapchat is being used by younger real estate agents to market themselves and their properties. Agents can create fun and entertaining Snaps featuring their listings and open houses. They can film and narrate ten second videos (with an Iphone hack available to bypass the time limit) and post them throughout the day. Snapchat is a very effective way to engage people and create a following. If you are in a market in which millennials are purchasing real estate, it is a great platform to include in your social media marketing strategy.

<u>Dustin Brohm</u>, an agent in Salt Lake City, Utah, is a big proponent of Snapchat. He has created an informative YouTube video, "How to Use Snapchat for Real Estate." Brohm uses Snapchat to acquire leads and referrals and to build his presence in the Salt Lake City market. He says that there are also indirect benefits of becoming proficient at making Snapchat videos: *"I've learned to be concise and to be comfortable in front of a camera. This has served me well when I give listing presentations."*

<u>Note</u>: The popularity and dominance of certain platforms can suddenly change, as new sites and new apps emerge and new technologies proliferate. For example, <u>Twitter</u>, the 280 character microblogging service, was once hot, but its growth has stalled dramatically in the last few years; it is now used mostly for news and links to other platforms.

**What if you don't have the time or the interest to create
and maintain an online presence?**

There are social media consultants and strategists who you can hire on an hourly, monthly, or project basis to help you develop and implement a strategy and maintain your online presence. You can also have a member of your team or a college student or intern take over your social media (with your input and supervision) to keep postings current.

Keeping Your Website Relevant and Timely

Most people begin their real estate search online. Therefore, your website needs to be up-to-date, well designed and well written. Make sure that your site looks great on mobile devices, as people are increasingly using smartphones and tablets for real estate searches. Put your name and phone number on each page of your website so that people can contact you easily.

> **Jerri:** Websites can cost from about $1500 to "the sky's the limit" (i.e., $100,000 or more) to design and build. Hosting is an additional monthly fee. There are a number of templates you can use to design your own website, or you can hire a web designer or a dedicated real estate website design firm and have a site custom-designed to your specifications. Generally, custom-designed websites start at around $5000.

Some online website design services worth exploring are listed below. _Note that we are not endorsing any providers; these are just suggestions to get you started_.

- <u>WIX</u> is a free, easy-to-use website builder with customizable templates for real estate agents and agencies, as well as for other professionals, businesses and nonprofits.
- <u>RealEstateDesigner</u> offers "premium" real estate website templates. The service is provided on a monthly fee basis.
- <u>RealtyTech</u> is another "premium" agent website design service offering package rates.

- <u>AgentImage</u> offers three levels of design: templates, semi-customizable, and fully custom-designed sites.

- <u>RealEstateWebmasters</u> is a high-end service offering web design, lead generation, and CRM.

- <u>RockhopperMediaGroup</u> provides custom real estate marketing, including website design, print marketing and digital magazines.

- <u>BoomtownRoi</u> is a real estate platform that includes website design, online lead generation, CRM technology and a mobile app. It offers a blog, library and podcast for agents. Costs range from $1000 to $30,000 a month, depending upon the size and scope of the business.

Before you spend any money and hire your own web designer or firm, look at a number of other agents' sites to see what you like and don't like about their designs. Decide what "look and feel" you want for your site. <u>Photos and videos</u> (including 3D virtual tours) <u>are now more important than text</u>. Make sure your site has MLS-IDX integration (integrated data exchange or broker reciprocity) so that your MLS data are automatically published on your own website.

Include testimonials from buyers and sellers with whom you've done business. To solicit testimonials you can send a personal letter or an email with a few questions, including: *"What was it like working with me as your agent?" "How would you describe the level of service you received?"* Follow up with a phone call or a text if you don't receive a response. Get permission before publishing quotes on your website and in other marketing materials.

Keep your website timely and updated. There's nothing worse than seeing expired listings, names and pictures of associates no longer on your team, or stale postings of "upcoming" seminars on a website. Hire a professional—either a virtual assistant, social media manager, or website designer—or have your assistant or a team member (or even a college student) keep your website up to date.

Developing and Protecting Your Brand

Jerri: Recently I watched several YouTube videos of people rapping about their expertise as Realtors®. Now, I'm not an expert in rap, but it seemed to me that none of them had any talent as rappers. Worse yet, I was extremely embarrassed by their performances. The agents, however, presumably thought that this was a good way to brand themselves. They certainly differentiated themselves from other agents, but did these videos showcase their experience and their competency?

As you grow your business, think about how you want to be viewed by your prospective clientele and by the public in general.

Ken: People are always judging you. You are never "off."

Be aware of how you are perceived by others—and how you want to be perceived. What image do you want to project? Do you want to be known for your knowledge and experience in the luxury market? As an expert agent for first-time buyers? As a philanthropist in the community who also has his/her pulse on the market?

Your advertising and marketing materials, your website and your social media postings should reflect the image you want to convey and also highlight your expertise, your niche, and your areas of specialization (if applicable). Design your advertising to appeal to the type of clientele you want to attract. Ads on grocery shopping carts or on-screen at movie theaters will be effective in certain markets; advertising at polo matches or in symphony orchestra programs will be effective in others.

Your image goes beyond your advertising and marketing efforts. It includes the way you dress, your demeanor, and how articulate you are in your texts and emails.

By now, most people are aware of the power of social media, and how important it is to make sure that you only post photos and comments that are appropriate. But how intelligible are your emails and texts? Are they written in such a hurry that they are replete with typos and grammatical errors? These, too, are part of the image that you are projecting, whether intentional or not.

Ken: People do stupid things. Make sure you protect your image and your brand. Think before you hit "post" or "send."

Key Takeaways

- There are many different ways to market yourself. You can
    - Expand your sphere of influence
    - Stay connected to past buyers and sellers
    - Ask for business—this includes referrals
    - Use social media.
- Keep your website relevant and timely.
- Develop and protect your brand.
- Get out of the office and talk to people. <u>Just do it</u>!

CHAPTER 6

<u>Putting It All Together:</u>
<u>Designing and Implementing Your</u>
<u>Business and Marketing Plan</u>

If you've completed all of the exercises up to this point, you have spent a fair amount of time learning about yourself and about your business. And you've explored ways to build upon what's working and to change what is not. **Well done! Thank you for challenging yourself and for being honest with yourself.**

If you haven't yet completed the exercises, now is the time to go back and do so before you proceed to the final steps in Part I: Creating a Great Business.

In this chapter you will review the work that you've done so far and <u>design</u> a business and marketing plan <u>that will work for you</u>, based upon your strengths and interests, your past successes, and your business goals. First, you will create three short-term (non-marketing) business objectives, and then three longer-term marketing strategies that you want to implement.

Exercise - Creating Your Short-Term
(Non-Marketing) Business Objectives

Go back to page 19 and write down the <u>five specific goals</u> that you want to achieve for your business within the next twelve months.

1.

2.

3.

4.

5.

Using these goals as a basis, write down three <u>non-marketing business</u> objectives that you want to implement within the next six months.

Then, for each objective <u>list the action steps</u> required to carry out that objective and the <u>date</u> by which you will have taken each step. Put each deadline on your calendar.

Examples:

Objective 1: Find an agent for reciprocal backup coverage by (date).

Action steps:	1. *Think about the type of person I am seeking. Write a list of the qualities of my ideal candidate.*	*By date*
	2. *Ask my manager for suggestions.*	*By date*
	3. *Meet with agents.*	*By date*

Objective 2: Hire a new accountant by (date).

Action steps:	1. *Ask colleagues for referrals.*	*By date*
	2. *Interview accountants.*	*By date*
	3. *Choose accountant.*	*By date*

Objective 3: Obtain the CRS designation by (date).

Action steps:	1. *Research upcoming courses.*	*By date*
	2. *Review my schedule.*	*By date*
	3. *Choose a course and enroll.*	*By date*

Objective 1. _____

        Action Steps: Action Step Deadlines:

1.   _____

2.   _____

3.   _____

4.   _____

5.   _____

Objective 2. _____

        Action Steps: Action Step Deadlines:

1.   _____

2.   _____

3.   _____

4.   _____

5.   _____

Objective 3. _____

      Action Steps: Action Step Deadlines:

1.   _____

2.   _____

3.   _____

4.   _____

5.   _____

Your Marketing Plan

Now go back to pages 38-39 and re-state your answers to the following questions:

- Which specific actions or strategies are generating <u>most</u> of your business?

    1.

    2.

    3.

    4.

    5.

- Who or what are the <u>top three sources of referrals</u> for your business?

    1.

    2.

    3.

- Which activities are generating <u>the least amount</u> of business and are draining your time and/or financial resources?

    1.

    2.

    3.

- Which <u>creative marketing strategies</u> on pages 52 to 63 are most appealing, interesting, and/or useful to you?

  1.

  2.

  3.

  4.

  5.

- Based on all of your answers above, <u>create three long-term</u> marketing strategies that you are willing (and eager!) to do.

- Write them below.

- Then, for each strategy, <u>list the action steps</u> required to carry out that strategy and <u>the date</u> by which you will have taken each step. Put each deadline on your calendar.

Examples:

- *<u>Strategy A: Create a Facebook business page and post weekly</u>.*

  Action steps: 1. Research social media strategists.   By <u>date</u>

  2. Learn about FB ad campaigns.   By <u>date</u>

  3. Hire strategist and develop a plan. By <u>date</u>

  4. Hire assistant to post.   By <u>date</u>

  4. And so on...

- _Strategy B: Send cards and chocolates for ____ (an upcoming holiday)._

      Action steps: 1. *Make a list of recipients.*   By _date_

                  2. *Gather addresses.*   By _date_

                  3. *Choose a gift vendor.*   By _date_

- _Strategy C: Take one referral partner out for coffee or lunch the first Tuesday of each month._

      Action steps: 1. *Block out the dates.*   By _date_

                  2. *Make a list of people to invite.* By _date_

                  3. *Schedule the first two meetings.* By _date_

Again, the keys are to choose activities <u>that you will actually do</u>, to schedule them on your calendar, and to be consistent in following through.

Strategy A. _____

      Action Steps: Action Step Deadlines:

1.   _____

2.   _____

3.   _____

4.   _____

5.   _____

Strategy B. _____

     Action Steps: Action Step Deadlines:

1.   _____

2.   _____

3.   _____

4.   _____

5.   _____

Strategy C. _____

     Action Steps: Action Step Deadlines:

1.   _____

2.   _____

3.   _____

4.   _____

5.   _____

It is <u>vital</u> that you create a system to follow up and follow through on your business objectives and marketing strategies.

Create a system using your paper calendar, your computer or your smartphone to remind you to follow up and follow through. This will ensure that you stay on track – even when you are at your busiest.

<u>Taking action–implementing your plans and following up with prospects–is key to success</u>. There is no point in generating leads, for example, and then letting them wither among your emails or in a pile on your desk.

The Power of a Single Daily Action

The phrase "single daily action" is a term that Thomas Leonard, one of the pioneers of the coaching profession, popularized. It means <u>do something every day</u> to move you toward your goals.

While you are growing your business, it is important to <u>take action every single day</u> in the direction of what you want.

Even if it's only twenty minutes of calls to prospects or two minutes to send a text on your day off, the actions you take will help you <u>maintain your momentum</u> and inhibit you from procrastinating. (If you are taking action <u>every single day</u>, there's no way you can put off a task "til tomorrow.") If you take the most difficult actions <u>first thing every day</u>, you will get them out of the way and begin your day feeling very productive.

Summary: Your Plan

- You have articulated your values and your purpose in being in real estate sales;
- You have discovered your top strengths;

- You have written your top five business goals for the next twelve months;

- You have figured out which actions or strategies are currently producing the most business for you; and

- You have created three short-term business objectives and three long-term marketing strategies that you are going to implement, with accompanying action steps and deadlines for each objective and for each strategy.

> **Congratulations! You've just designed your business and marketing plan—your blueprint for success!**

Exercise - Finalizing Your Business and Marketing Plan

Now, go to the Blueprint for Success (pages 149 through 156) and, on the first worksheet, copy
- your values (from page 12),

- your purpose (from page 14),

- your top ten strengths (from pages 32-33),

- your business goals (from page 19),

- your short-term business objectives, action steps and deadlines (from pages 68-69); and

- your long-term marketing strategies, action steps and deadlines (from pages 72-73).

Note that there are three copies of the Blueprint so that you can revise your plan periodically as your goals manifest and/or change.

Creating a Budget

As an independent sales agent you are the CEO and CFO (as well as the Chief Marketing Officer) of your business. As such, you are responsible for generating the income and incurring the expenses of your operation.

When you first started in business you may have had as much as a six month delay between the time you began as a sales agent and the time you received your first commission check. You may also have had a shock when you met with your accountant and discovered how much you owed in quarterly estimated federal, state, and perhaps even city tax payments.

Now that you've been in business for a while, you have most likely developed an annual budget and a system for accruing funds to pay your taxes and save money for the future. <u>It's important that you include marketing expenses in your budget</u>.

Below are suggested budget categories for your business. Be sure to expand and/or modify these based upon your business needs and your marketing plan.

<u>General Business Expenses</u>
Salaries (include employer's share of taxes, worker's compensation, benefits)
Occasional/hourly help/office assistance
Consultants (legal, accounting, business coaching, tech support, social media, website design)
Referral fees
Transaction fees
Auto (loan or lease payments, insurance, gas, repairs, tolls and parking)
Office supplies, furniture and equipment
Software
Postage
Bank fees
Telephone and internet
Dues and license fees
Books and subscriptions

Errors & omissions insurance, liability insurance
Professional training, conferences, CEUs
Other business travel
Charitable contributions

Property Expenses
Advertising
Signage
Staging, floor plans, photography, videography
Brochure design
Open house expenses
Smoke detectors

Marketing and Advertising Expenses
Meals and entertainment
Marketing events
Promotional items
Client gifts
Printing expenses
Mailing expenses
Lead generation system expenses
Print ads
Website design, hosting and maintenance
Social media advertising

Other
Taxes
Savings
Retirement funding

This list is fairly comprehensive. But one thing is missing....YOU NEED TO PAY YOURSELF FIRST! Make sure that there is a line item for your own "draw" as an independent contractor.

If the above list is daunting, make an appointment with your accountant to review the last several years' worth of numbers and create a budget for the next twelve months. Be sure to review both your income and your expenses <u>on an ongoing basis</u> so you can plan appropriately.

<u>You need to know your numbers</u> so that you can see where you are in relation to your goals.

Jerri: People who work for themselves can fall into a financial trap. Monthly—and often yearly—income can vary greatly, as markets rise and fall, interest rates fluctuate, seasons change, and other factors come into play. If you fall into the trap of adopting a lifestyle based upon your highest months or years of income, you will have difficulty maintaining that lifestyle if business slows down and your income falls. And the stress to produce will become intolerable.

We hope this book will provide you with the tools and resources to use so that you can even out the cycles. Still, it is important to develop the discipline to maintain a lifestyle that can be supported by the lower range of your income. When you have great months or years, the additional income can be saved or invested and used in the future to supplement slower months.

Key Takeaways

- Your business goals, your strengths, your interests and your past successes are the chief considerations when designing your business and marketing plan.

- Marketing strategies need to include specific action steps (with deadlines) that you are committed to taking.

- Create a system of reminders to ensure that you stay on track and meet your deadlines.

- A detailed budget for your business should include marketing expenses and take into consideration your "draw," as well as federal, state and other taxes and savings for retirement.

CHAPTER 7

Guiding Principles: Commitment, Accountability, and Legal and Ethical Standards

Principle 1: Don't Give Up on Yourself: The Power of Commitment

> **"There are only two options regarding commitment. You're either in or you're out. There is no such thing as life in-between."**
> – Pat Riley, Hall of Fame basketball coach

The word "commitment" is synonymous with dedication, perseverance and promise. Commitment is the difference between a "good idea" in your head and "fire in your belly." It is the drive, the focus and the passion that enable you to keep moving forward despite the inevitable setbacks, obstacles and frustrations that come with this challenging business. It is what psychologist Angela Duckworth calls "grit"—the power of passion and perseverance that is "the secret to outstanding achievement."

When you are "all-in," committed to yourself and to achieving what you want, you are fully engaged. People around you can sense your energy and your focus, and they want to work with you and spend time with you. Conversely, without this full commitment you are just going through the motions, and you will have difficulty creating the results you desire.

Ken: I had been working with an agent in my office for quite a while. He had had a failed business, been divorced, and decided to begin a career in real estate at age 50+. For the first five or six months he stumbled and struggled. I finally told him, *"Let's not make this a struggle. You have to find some sort of fun in the job. You have to find elements that are positive and joyful, even though you are depressed. Otherwise this job will eat you up.*

"And you either need to sink or swim. You need to <u>commit</u> to this. Talk without action is meaningless."

This conversation was pivotal for the agent. After our coaching session he re-committed to his new career and decided to specialize in listings in his own condominium complex. He became the expert and go-to-agent in his building. He is now on his way to a substantial income.

Ken: You can't give up on yourself–ever. When your competitor gets the listing you worked so hard to obtain, when your home inspection reveals structural damage, when your latest deal falls apart–what do you do?

Jerri: Here's a great, empowering technique based on one that I learned from Robert Fritz a number of years ago:

First, give yourself permission to be angry and upset–whether for a few hours or even a few days. Break a few plates, pound your pillow, maybe even do a "silent scream" or two in your car or in the bathroom.

Then, after you've vented long enough, step back, take a few deep breaths, and let your feelings go. Ask yourself: *"What do I really want right now?"* and answer the question honestly. The answer might be *"a peaceful resolution of the issue,"* or it might be *"a new $500,000 sale, with all parties who are reasonable and easy to work with,"* or it might be *"I need to take a short vacation and focus on my own needs."*

Whatever the answer, <u>commit to this goal</u> and visualize it coming to you. Then move on. Go for a walk, put on some music and dance, read a book. <u>Just change the energy</u>.

Ken: Get your feelings out without bringing them into the office or dumping them on your partner. You need to be responsible for your emotions and your reactions. It is better to vent in private so as not to damage your relationships. Venting is cathartic, but it doesn't create a solution. What is more effective is refocusing and recommitting to your goal.

Commitment is <u>powerful</u>. It will help propel you forward toward what you want.

Exercise - Your Commitment

How committed are you to taking the action steps you've outlined in your plan? (0 being "not committed at all" to 10 being "fully committed") _____

How committed are you to achieving your goals? (0 to 10) _____

What would it take for you to become fully committed (if you are not already)?

_____

Are you willing to do what it takes? _____

Principle 2: Staying on Track: The Importance of Accountability

To be accountable is to be responsible, to make sure <u>that you actually do</u> what you say you are going to do. This is one of the benefits of coaching: having someone outside of yourself holding you accountable for your actions, supporting you in fulfilling your commitments to yourself and to others.

"Accountability helps keep (people) on track...As coaches, we hold clients accountable...to empower them in making the changes they want to make," write Whitworth, et al. in *Co-Active Coaching: New Skills for Coaching People Toward Success in Work and Life.*

There are both <u>inner</u> and <u>outer</u> commitments and expectations, and different people respond differently to each type. (Inner commitments are <u>self-imposed</u>, such as beginning an exercise program or giving up caffeine; outer expectations are <u>externally imposed</u>, such as meeting work deadlines or paying your mortgage on time.)

Gretchen Rubin, author of *Better Than Before: Mastering the Habits of Our Everyday Lives*, has studied the nature of habits and developed what she terms *"the four tendencies,"* a framework for describing *"how (people) respond to expectations."*

According to Rubin, there are four tendencies:

- <u>Upholders</u> - who *"respond readily to both outer expectations and inner expectations;"*
- <u>Questioners</u> - who *"question all expectations, and will meet an expectation only if they believe it's justified;"*
- <u>Obligers</u> - who *"respond readily to outer expectations but struggle to meet inner expectations;"* and
- <u>Rebels</u> - who *"resist all expectations, outer and inner alike."*

Most people are either Questioners or Obligers, and it is Obligers who benefit the most from outside accountability.

To discover which category you fall into, take the free, simple test at www.gretchenrubin.com (search "the four tendencies quiz").

In order to ensure that you follow through on your business plan (especially if you are an Obliger), you can

- hire a professional business coach,

- team up with an accountability partner,

- join an accountability or mastermind group, or

- meet with your manager on a regular basis for support.

People find these approaches to be extremely helpful and effective in making sure that they stay on track.

Jerri: Coaching is one of the best ways to help people move forward in their lives and to remain accountable for what they say they want to achieve. As a coach, I partner with my clients to help them reach their goals. My job is to help them clarify what they want, to act as a sounding board, to provide a fresh perspective on challenges and opportunities, and to offer strategies and solutions, when asked.

Coaching is not therapy. It is about creating, strategizing and implementing a plan, setting goals, and acting to make them real. Many top-producing real estate agents, managers, CEOs, entrepreneurs and star athletes hire coaches to help them maximize their potential and create more meaningful lives.

Coaches can serve as accountability partners. I often remind clients of what they have said they wanted to achieve when they have lost sight of their goals in the heat of the moment. It is indeed a special relationship, and at its best is extremely rewarding and gratifying for both the client and the coach.

Exercise - How Will You Remain Accountable?

Into which of the four tendencies categories do you fall?

_____

How will you remain accountable so that you can stay focused on your goals?

_____

Principle 3: Do the Right Thing: Legal and Ethical Standards

You are a licensed real estate salesperson or broker in your state, and, as such, are bound by the laws and regulations of the state in which you are licensed. You are also bound by both the federal Fair Housing Act (Title VIII of the Civil Rights Act of 1968) and its 1988 amendment which prohibit discrimination in the sale, rental and financing of dwellings based on race, color, religion, sex, national origin, disability or familial status (i.e., the presence of a child under the age of 18, and pregnant women).

If you are also a Realtor® (i.e., a member of the National Association of Realtors®) you are bound by the NAR Code of Ethics and Standards of Practice (www. nar.realtor/code-of-ethics). Needless to say, you should periodically review federal and state laws and regulations and the Code of Ethics and Standards of Practice to stay up-to-date and to remind yourself of all of your obligations.

These laws, regulations, codes and standards detail, among many other requirements, your obligations to clients, including conflicts of interest, misrepresentations, anti-discrimination regulations, and dispute resolution.

While it is not the purpose of this book to outline the legal and ethical duties and obligations of real estate agents, we do want to reiterate several points that you should have learned.

- If a referral is not from a licensed real estate broker or a properly licensed party, it may well be unlawful for you to pay anyone compensation (such as a fee or commission) for any reason.

- Taking a referral agent to lunch or sending her or him a small thank you gift may or may not be permitted. You should check with your own attorney or real estate board if you have any questions about this or about all other legal and ethical conflicts, as the laws vary by state.

- The Real Estate Settlement Procedures Act (RESPA) of 1974 (Section 12) prohibits, among other things, *"kickbacks and unearned fees,"* particularly in connection with federally related mortgage loans. Note specifically: *"Any person who gives or accepts a fee, kickback, or thing of value (payments, commissions, gifts, tangible item, or special privileges) for the referral of settlement business is in violation of Section 8(a) of RESPA."*

Why is this relevant to you, the sales agent? If you are the recipient of a fee, kickback or something "of value" from a mortgage broker, loan officer, title company officer, escrow agent or attorney (including a closing attorney), you may well be in violation of RESPA (and other laws) and be subject to stiff penalties and liabilities.

If you have questions about RESPA, contact your managing broker or attorney.

It is always best to do the right thing. It is also your obligation. Otherwise, you could be subject to severe penalties, including the loss of your license. If you undertake an illegal act or unethical practice, you will always be looking over your shoulder and second-guessing yourself. Why put yourself in that position?

It's impossible to create a great business and have a life you love without conducting your business in a legal and ethical manner and holding yourself to the highest possible standards.

Key Takeaways

- Commitment has great power. It keeps you motivated and focused on your goals.

- Different people respond to inner and outer commitments and expectations differently. Being accountable to someone else can help you stay on track.

- It is important to conduct yourself and your business in a legal and ethical manner, holding yourself to the highest possible standards. Periodically review federal and state laws and regulations and the NAR Code of Ethics and Standards of Practice to stay up-to-date.

Before you begin Part II...

You are now almost half-way through the book. If you haven't completed all of the exercises in Part I (or if you've skimmed or skipped over chapters), we suggest that you make the time and go back and do the necessary work, even if it takes you several weeks to do so.

> **Ken:** Success doesn't happen overnight. It takes time and dedication. If you haven't finished the exercises, take a look and see how your business and your life might mirror that. Where are there incompletions in your life? Where do you take short cuts that affect the quality of the results you produce?

If you have diligently completed the work, congratulations. Well done! Now it's time to move on to Part II: Creating a Life You Love.

Part II

Creating a Life You Love

CHAPTER 8

How to Create a Life You Love

**"Tell me, what is it you plan to do
with your one wild and precious life?"**
– From "The Summer Day" by Pulitzer Prize-winning poet Mary Oliver

**"Do not expect work to fill a void that non-work
relationships and activities should."**
– Tim Ferriss, author of *The 4-Hour Workweek*

Questions to ponder:

- Have you ever cancelled dinner plans with friends in order to meet with clients to write up an offer?

- Are you neglecting your most important relationships by spending excessive amounts of money rather than enough time on those you love?

- Have you ever forgotten to call a good friend on his birthday because you were too busy holding an open house?

- Are you filling up your time with work and then coming home feeling drained and empty?

- Are you married to your real estate business rather than to your partner?

Ken: Real estate can be a substitute for a full, healthy life. But your clients aren't necessarily your friends. When your birthday or the holidays arrive, your clients aren't there for you the same way that a partner or friends will be.

Jerri: Having a life you love includes having friends who are not just conduits to more business. It means having people with whom you can be yourself, with whom you can exchange confidences, share a laugh or a good cry, and relax…where's there's no hidden agenda.

What's most important to you?

Jerri:

- My client Rebecca, a manager at a corporate headquarters, wanted to become more physically fit. She decided to take up bodybuilding and, with my encouragement, hired a trainer and trained for an upcoming competition. Although she didn't win the contest, her physical transformation was remarkable. As she wrote me: *"Getting fit, 'getting my body back' and becoming an athlete again have meant the world to me….Mostly I feel alive and more able to tackle what life has in store. I have more energy <u>and</u> I have more balance. You helped make this become a reality and helped my dreams come true."*

- A real estate agent I worked with wrote me, *"You might like to know that I've just returned from Ireland. It was great! And I've gotten good feedback on the person who covered for me. Thanks for everything."*

- And this from a broker client who put an indoor lap pool in her house: *"I was thrilled to show (my house renovations) to you. I have a great place to live and a great place to work. I thank you for your support in bringing about both. I know you help most people create more balance in their lives. I'm just a workaholic who doesn't want much more balance. But hey, I got a pool :)"*

Ken: In our work we take a holistic—and realistic—approach to the subject of balance. Life cannot be totally in balance at all times. Sometimes you need to put more attention in one domain, such as on your business. Sometimes you need to put more attention in another, such as on your relationship or on your health.

Like nature, human beings are always in flux. Complete balance and perfection are only for glossy magazine features. They portray a fantasy that is rarely obtainable.

What would a life <u>you love</u> look like?

In coaching the "whole agent," we often suggest that a client's goals include areas outside of career and finances: significant other/romance; friends and family; health; home environment; fun, play and recreation; creative expression; and personal growth.

The exercise below will enable you to discover just what is most important to you.

Exercise - Creating Life Goals

(Note that this exercise is based on one created by The Coaches Training Institute called "The Wheel of Life.")

For each of the following categories, rate your <u>level of satisfaction</u> on a scale of 1 to 10, 1 being "completely unsatisfied" and 10 being "completely satisfied."

Significant other/romance   _____

Friends and family   _____

Health   _____

Home environment   _____

Fun, play and recreation   _____

Creative expression   _____

Personal growth   _____

Other _____

Now, choose (mark or highlight) three categories on which you want to focus. They could be the categories with the lowest ratings or the ones that appeal to you the most. Create a <u>goal</u> for each of these categories, writing your goals <u>in the present tense</u>.

Examples:

- *I am meditating daily.*
- *I am redecorating my bedroom and creating a space I really love.*
- *I have a charming cabin in the woods overlooking a lake that is the perfect weekend retreat for my family and me.*

Make sure that your goals are <u>specific</u>, <u>unambiguous</u>, and <u>measurable</u>, and are results you <u>truly</u> want for yourself. Choose goals that are <u>worth doing</u>.

Write three life goals in the spaces below:

1. _____

2. _____

3. _____

Then, under each goal, write a brief description of what you are <u>doing</u> and how you are <u>feeling</u> as you accomplish that goal.

Finally, sit in a quiet place and, if you want, close your eyes. In your mind, picture yourself having achieved each one of these goals.

<u>Do this exercise daily, in the morning and before bedtime, for the next few weeks</u>.

Taking Action Toward Your Life Goals

Once you are clear about your goals and have begun visualizing yourself having achieved them, you will <u>naturally</u> take steps toward their fulfillment. You may notice interesting coincidences, inner urgings that prompt you to take actions in unexpected ways, unusual (and perfect) advice from friends, and other signs that you are moving closer to what you want.

It will also be useful for you to create

- some <u>specific action steps</u>—so that you can reach your goals faster and more effectively;

- a <u>budget</u>—so that you can see how these goals will impact you financially; and

- an <u>estimate</u> of <u>how much time</u> it will take you either to

  - <u>engage</u> in the project (e.g., take tango lessons or meditate daily); or to

  - <u>accomplish</u> the goal (e.g., renovate your home office)—so that you can schedule your time accordingly.

Exercise - Creating an Action Plan
for Your Life Goals

1. Copy your <u>first</u> life goal (from page 94).

_____

2. <u>List three or more action steps below</u> that will either help you make significant progress toward your goal or enable you to accomplish it. <u>Create deadlines for each step</u>.

Examples:

- <u>Your goal is to take a vacation to Hawaii</u> with your family.

Action steps: 1. Schedule the trip.   *By <u>date</u>*

2. Arrange backup for your business.   *By <u>date</u>*

3. Research hotels, flights and activities. *By <u>date</u>*

4. And so on…

- <u>Your goal is to have a date night or evening out with your partner and/or friends each Friday night</u>.

	Action steps:		By When:
Action steps:	*1. Schedule the dates.*		*By <u>date</u>*
	2. Plan the activities.		*By <u>date</u>*
	3. Arrange a babysitter.		*By <u>date</u>*

<u>Action steps:</u>   <u>By When:</u>

1.

2.

3.

4.

5.

<u>Make sure you put each deadline on your calendar.</u>

3. Next, create a <u>budget</u> for the goal, if appropriate. Obviously, some goals (such as beginning a meditation practice or taking a photography class) will not have significant costs associated with them, while others (such as renovating your home office or taking an overseas vacation) will. If appropriate, you may want to increase the financial goal you created for your business on page 19 to cover the additional costs of this life goal. Budget for the goal: $ _____

4. Finally, estimate how much time it will take either to accomplish the goal or to engage in the project: _____ hours per _____.

1. Copy your <u>second</u> life goal (from page 95).

_____

2. List <u>three or more action steps</u> that will either help you make significant progress toward the goal or enable you to accomplish it. Create deadlines for each step below.

       <u>Action steps:</u>   <u>By When:</u>

1.

2.

3.

4.

5.

3. Create a budget for the goal, if appropriate. $ _____

4. Estimate how much time it will take either to accomplish this goal or to engage in the project: _____ hours per _____.

1. Copy your <u>third</u> life goal (from page 95).

_____

2. List three or more action steps below. Create deadlines for each step.

<u>Action steps</u>:   <u>By When</u>:

1.

2.

3.

4.

5.

3. Create a <u>budget</u> for the goal, if appropriate.

$ _____

4. Estimate how much time it will take either to accomplish this goal or to engage in the project: _____ hours per _____.

Copy these goals, action steps and deadlines on pages 155-156 of the Blueprint for Success so you can refer to them easily.

Key Takeaways

- Real estate should not be a substitute for a full, satisfying life.

- Become clear on what you want in your non-work life. This is key to creating a life you love.

- You can use the same techniques to create a great life that you use to create a successful business.

- To create a life you love:

  - State your goals in the present tense;

  - Visualize what your life looks and feels like when you have achieved each goal; and

  - Create an action plan with action steps, deadlines and a budget, as appropriate.

(Optional) CHAPTER 9

How to Create an Intimate Relationship

"A deep sense of love and belonging is an irreducible need of all people. We are biologically, cognitively, physically, and spiritually wired to love, to be loved, and to belong. When those needs are not met, we don't function as we were meant to. We break. We fall apart. We numb. We ache...We get sick.

"Connection is why we're here; it is what gives purpose and meaning to our lives."
– Research Professor Brené Brown, Ph.D.

Jerri: There's a question that I occasionally ask in my coaching sessions: *"What's the use of making an extra twenty-five, fifty, or one hundred thousand dollars if you have no one to cuddle with?"*

This point was brought home when I was watching the reality television show, "Million Dollar Listing - New York." One of the super-star agents, Luis D. Ortiz, an effervescent, high-energy broker, had just closed a huge sale and made a $450,000 commission.

When he got back to his apartment he teared up as he told the camera how upset he was that he had no one with whom to share his success. (He subsequently left New York to pursue other interests that would bring him *"more joy,"* and perhaps also to make time to find a relationship.)

For some agents it's easy to focus all of their energies on work, an arena that brings them great success, financial rewards and well regard. Work is also an area that does not require the same vulnerabilities and emotional investment as does an intimate relationship.

Yet the deep levels of love, satisfaction, happiness and belonging that most people seek are best found in healthy intimate relationships, in close friendships, and in a rich family life—not in client and customer interactions.

In coaching agents, we have noticed that some people say they want an intimate relationship, but then put all of their time, attention and energy into work, leaving no room for finding and developing a life partnership. Others put tremendous focus and attention into creating a large circle of friends and acquaintances, filling their time with a frenetic social life—and leaving no space for a partner to enter.

Jerri: Your ability to find love is predicated upon your having <u>at least as strong a commitment</u> to your personal life as it is to growing your business.

Exercise - Creating an Intimate Relationship

- Write a complete <u>detailed</u> description of your ideal partner: the qualities, a full physical description of him or her, and so forth. Think about what <u>didn't</u> work about previous relationships and write the <u>opposite</u> on your list.

  Make sure to include characteristics such as *"totally monogamous and committed to me"* (if that's what you want), *"similar values and interests," "healthy," "fun to be around," "likes to travel to interesting places with me,"* and so forth.

- Write a <u>description</u> of what it looks and feels like when you are in this relationship—what you are doing, how you are feeling, and so on.

- <u>What you are telling yourself</u> about achieving this life goal? Do you say, for example, *"I can never have a great relationship."* *"This is too difficult."* *"I don't deserve to have this."*?

- <u>What do you believe</u> about creating this goal? Do you believe, *"I'm super-successful in the business domain, but I can never have _____."* Or *"It's too hard to _____."*?

- Change any negative self-talk and self-beliefs to ones that support you: *"I am attracting love."* *"I am in a great relationship with the perfect partner."* *"I have a balanced, happy life that I love."* *"<u>I can have this!</u>"*

- Next, ask yourself: *"How committed am I to achieving this goal?"* If you are not totally committed, then ask yourself: *"What would it take for me to become <u>totally committed</u> to my goal?"*

- Commit to your goal (if you are able), and visualize yourself having achieved it. *What are you and your partner doing together? Where are you going? How does it feel when you are together?*

- Do this visualization twice a day, first thing in the morning and before going to sleep at night.

- Read your description of your ideal partner daily, and revise and expand the list as you see fit.

- Again, follow any inner promptings and inklings, especially those that lead you to <u>take action in different ways</u> from your usual, habitual behaviors.

If you want to create a new and different result, you need to take new and different actions.

The Symbolic Gesture

A symbolic gesture is an action you take that represents the outcome you desire. It has *"a greater meaning because of what it represents."*

Jerri: When I coach clients who want to create an intimate relationship, I often suggest that they <u>consciously</u> make space in their lives for someone to enter. This means creating time in their schedules as well as space in their homes. As a symbolic gesture that represents you living with your ideal partner (if that's what you want), you might empty a dresser drawer for him or her, make room in your closet, buy two champagne flutes or coffee mugs, or add pictures to your vision board of you and this person on a romantic vacation. (Note: use an image from a magazine, <u>not</u> a photo of a <u>specific</u> person you know.)

Exercise - The Symbolic Gesture

List one or two symbolic gestures you will make which represent your being in an intimate relationship.

Key Takeaways

- Creating an intimate relationship uses the same techniques you've learned to create other goals.

- This requires a strong commitment to having a partner in your life, including making time and space for the relationship.

- To create a new and different result you need to take new and different actions.

Part III

Tips from Top Producers:
Seven Keys to Success

Jerri: The Seven Keys to Success discussed in this Part are based on responses to a survey of top-producing agents that Janet Reilly, a real estate coach and manager, and I conducted at a large agency in Boston a number of years ago, before cell phones, texting and social media became ubiquitous. Ken and I have subsequently updated and expanded the list of keys to make them more relevant, addressing issues facing agents today.

Key 1: Provide Extraordinary Service

According to a 2010 McKinsey report, a satisfied customer will tell <u>three</u> people about his positive experience with you within a <u>month</u>; an unhappy customer will tell <u>seven</u> people of a bad experience within a <u>week</u>.

Ken: When I was an agent I created my own "15 Day Program." I called sellers every day for ten days before each closing, asking *"what can I do?"* I also called them for five days after each closing to see if everything went well during the move and that they were happy in their new home.

One hot summer day I called Mary to check in while she was packing. She said, *"I would love an iced coffee."* So for ten days I called and asked, *"Is it time for an iced coffee?"* and I would stop by and drop one off.

Many years later, I am still in touch with Mary and her husband, and have continued to do business with her and her friends.

Real estate brokerage is a service business. Top producers are dedicated to excellence. They put in long hours and <u>consistently</u> provide extraordinary service to their clients and customers. <u>They exceed expectations</u>. This means

- Keeping in frequent communication with current clientele;

- Responding to texts, emails and voice messages in a timely manner;

- Being an expert on your market (inventory, trends, interest rates, absorption rates, and the like);

- Honing your skills and knowledge (studying for a new real estate designation, taking a negotiation seminar or an architectural history class, embracing a new technology); and

- Doing more than is expected of you, so that your clients feel taken care of.

When you are working with buyers do you ever

- Schedule a coffee break between showings and buy your customers coffee and snacks at a local café?

- Provide local newspapers and other periodicals to your out-of-town customers?

- Suggest restaurants, sites and attractions that buyers might enjoy in your city or town?

- Provide refreshments or give out goodie bags at your open houses?

Do you ever

- Send flowers to clients on important occasions?

- Provide names of professional organizers, antique appraisers, consignment stores, handymen and other resources to help clients downsize?

- Bring or send dinner to clients on move-in day?

- Offer introductions to bankers, pre-school administrators and others, as appropriate?

Alexandra Conigliaro Biega, an agent in Back Bay, Boston, provides FaceTime video property tours to her out-of-state and international clients. *"There is no doubt that technology is changing residential real estate brokerage, allowing us to expand the level of service we offer. I think it is important for us to take advantage of the new, enhanced tools as they become available.*

"I often use FaceTime or video tours with out-of-town clients who are not able to attend showings. These tours enable clients to make decisions remotely. I had a client purchase a condo in Boston via a video tour while living in California. He never saw the unit in person until the closing, when he moved to Boston. I have also done this for a number of rental clients who were relocating.

"This really works, and I think it can help show clients that you are willing to go above and beyond to help them find the right place, no matter the circumstance."

Another great resource, especially for out-of-town buyers, is Matterport, a marketing platform providing HDR photos, floor plans, and 3D and virtual reality tours of listings online.

Cindy Lyon, a broker in Santa Fe, New Mexico, provides Matterport videos for all of her team's listings. She, too, has sold property to a buyer who had not visited the home prior to the sale.

"The buyer didn't walk into the house until the day after the closing. He had a level of confidence and trust in us that we wouldn't sell him a property that wouldn't be a good home for him. He was comfortable enough going through the house on Matterport that he went ahead with the transaction without actually coming to New Mexico.

"Online video tours are great for all buyers. They can preview properties before they get here and screen out ones that would be a waste of their time. Also, once someone has seen ten houses in a day, it's of great value to them to be able to re-experience the house."

Cindy shared a note from one of her sellers: *"Wow! You raised the standard of excellence! Your Matterport video made all the difference in marketing our home. No doubt that's what helped get us an offer in just 12 days. Thank you for all you did."*

Yes, that's extraordinary service!

Exercise - Providing Extraordinary Service

What are three ways you can enhance the level of service you provide?

1.

2.

3.

Key Takeaways

- Providing extraordinary service means exceeding expectations.
- Hard work, focus and drive are hallmarks of the top producer. So are knowledge, expertise, generosity, and attention to detail.

Key 2: Maximize Your Time

Jerri: Activity is not the same thing as productivity. Being <u>busy</u> is not the same as being <u>effective</u>.

We don't use the phrase "time management" in this book. One cannot "manage" time; at best, we can maximize our use of it. How you spend your time ought to reflect your goals and your priorities—what's most important to you. Sometimes the best use of your time is organizing your thoughts or reviewing your to-do list the night before work. Sometimes the best use of your time is to take a nap.

Chris Bailey, author of *A Life of Productivity*, has written, *"Today, productivity isn't about doing more, faster—it's about doing the right things, deliberately and intentionally. The more energy and focus we can bring to our work, the better."*

Real estate agents can be pulled in a million directions and easily lose focus.

**Spend your time on the business activities that will have
the biggest impact on your bottom line.**

<u>The two most important tasks in real estate sales are generating leads and following up on leads.</u> Top producers use their time to market themselves, obtain listings, selectively work with buyers, negotiate offers and resolve problems. Their assistants manage the details of the transactions so that agents are free to bring in more business.

Tips for Becoming More Organized and Productive

At last count, there were more than 60,000 books on time management on Amazon.com. If you are constantly running late, overbooking yourself, missing appointments, losing your keys or misplacing your phone, it would be worthwhile to read a book on this subject, hire a professional organizer, work with a coach, or take a seminar to help you learn to maximize your time.

There are a lot of tips and techniques to assist you. Here are some of the most useful:

- Block off time periods of one to two hours weekly or biweekly when you are unavailable by phone, text and email and cannot be interrupted. You can then work on projects requiring your sustained concentration, such as planning a new marketing campaign, calling past clients and customers or studying for a new real estate designation. <u>Schedule these time blocks for the time of day when you have the most energy</u>—your "internal prime time"—(probably not after lunch!). <u>Actually make an appointment with yourself,</u> and put it on your calendar. Treat this time period as seriously as if it were a listing appointment or an appointment with your physician.

Jerri: I recently got a note from a former client who I hadn't seen in many years: *"You were such a great influence when I was starting my business. You made some helpful points that have stayed with me during my successful 20+ year career. Knowing how to structure my day according to when I work best: creative work in the morning, invoicing in the afternoon, self-promotional writing when the muse hits, etc. For me, as a self-employed artist, this has made an enormous difference in structuring my time, increasing productivity and lowering my stress levels."* <u>Stephen Burdick</u>, graphic designer

---

Ken: I have five standing meetings (at the same time every week or every other week) with staff and agents. I have come to appreciate a recurring schedule and the structure that it provides. Recently I started taking Thursday afternoons from 3 to 4 pm for myself. I leave the office and go to a coffee shop nearby with my notebook and my one-line business journal. This is "think and reflect" time for me, when I review my thoughts from the prior week and make notes to myself. Having time without interruptions has really improved the quality of my work life.

Jerri: There are two signs that I put on my office door when I do not want to be interrupted. One says, "On a business call. Please do not disturb." The other says, "I am deep in thought. Please do not disturb." These work quite well.

- Use the time block technique to set aside time for yourself and for your own personal projects.

- "Eat the frog" – select the biggest, hardest, most important task first thing each morning. Get it done before moving on to something else.

- Group like tasks together (e.g., returning phone calls, running errands, and especially scheduling showings back-to-back).

- Create systems for staying on top of everything. Set up reminders on your smartphone for meetings and follow-up phone calls; use the "notes" feature to keep running lists of ideas, items to purchase, favorite wines, and so on.

Wil Catlin is the managing director and senior partner of a large commercial office leasing firm in downtown Boston. When asked about his time management techniques he said, *"How people manage emails is mission-critical. I get between 250 and 300 emails a day. I use the rules function within Outlook to automatically sort emails into folders so that I can focus on what's most important. If you don't have rules and boundaries set up, there will be chaos in your inbox."*

- Design and use checklists to manage transactions, so that important tasks and deadlines do not fall between the cracks. In the book *The Checklist Manifesto: How to Get Things Right*, author and surgeon Atul Gawande makes a compelling case for the use of checklists to enhance productivity.

- Limit your time on social media. One can easily spend hours a day on Facebook, Twitter, Instagram, Pinterest and more. Before you know it, the morning or afternoon is gone.

It is increasingly important to use social media to market yourself, your business and your properties. However, become <u>efficient</u> and <u>disciplined</u> so that this activity doesn't become a huge time waster.

There is an Iphone and Ipad app called Moment that allows you to track your screen time, including the total number of minutes spent on the phone and the time spent on various apps. You can set a daily limit on usage, and get notified when you've reached that limit.

Exercise - Becoming More Organized and Productive

List three ways in which you are going to become more organized and productive.

1.

2.

3.

Key Takeaways

- Being busy is not the same thing as being productive.

- Spend your time on the activities that will have the biggest impact on your business.

- Block off time periods in your schedule for uninterrupted work requiring sustained concentration.

- Create systems and use checklists to stay on top of everything.

- Limit your time on social media.

Key 3: Set Boundaries

"'No' is a complete sentence."
– Author Anne Lamott

"Whatever you are willing to put up with, is exactly what you will have."
– Anonymous

A boundary is something that indicates a border or a limit. Boundaries are key concepts in real estate: all property has borders that define it, and the deed to a property explicitly delineates these borders.

This is not necessarily so for the agent. Real estate brokerage is one of the few professions without fixed hours or a defined backup support system. With unlimited email and texting possibilities and the growing number of international clients, agents can be expected to be available 24/7/365.

If you want to have a great life outside of real estate (and prevent burnout), it is important to set boundaries with your clients, customers, other agents and staff.

Say something such as: *"I work x days a week, from x am to y pm, unless I'm negotiating an offer or there is an emergency."* By setting parameters up front, at the initial conversation, you are teaching your clients and customers about your availability.

Be wary of answering calls at 9 pm, if clients are just calling to chat. Unless you are negotiating an offer, nothing is so important that it can't wait until morning.

If you answer routine phone calls late at night, and return texts in the early hours of the morning, what are you telling/teaching your clients?

- <u>Wil Catlin</u>, the commercial broker in Boston quoted above, has an international clientele, many of whom work in very different time zones from his. They tend to call and text him at all hours of the day and night. Here is how Wil sets boundaries with his clients so that he is able to enjoy life with his family as well as take care of his clients:

"When I come home from work I take my phone and put it in my office (at the other end of the house) on vibrate mode. My phone does not come to the dinner table. I'm committed to spending that time—uninterrupted—with my family. I'm in the moment with my children and my wife. Everyone gets everyone else's undivided attention.

"After dinner I spend time in my office responding to texts and emails and getting ready for the next day. If I am organized it makes my life incredibly easy.

"I set expectations with my clients and associates and I honor them. I would never tell a client to just call me anytime. I would say, 'Call me whenever. I will get back to you when I have the time to do so.' I will talk to people seven days a week, at a mutually convenient time. All people really want is acknowledgment that something is happening, but I do triage what can wait."

Ken: Kerry was a top producer in my office for many years, until she retired and moved to another city. She generally did not hold open houses on weekends. She told me, *"I think that they are a waste of time. I feel that one-on-one showings are much more effective.*

"I set expectations at the beginning with sellers: I hold an open house the first week the property is on the market and then another one at the price reduction. You really don't have to work every weekend."

Exercise - Setting Time Boundaries

How much do you want to work? Specifically, when do you want to be available to clients, customers, other agents and staff each day? How much time do you want to take for yourself each week, and when?

In the space below, write down your designated "business hours." Then, for a week, keep track of the actual hours you've worked. See how closely they match your designated hours.

<u>Designated Business Hours</u>:   <u>Actual Hours Worked</u>:

Monday:

Tuesday:

Wednesday:

Thursday:

Friday:

Saturday:

Sunday:

Another boundary that you might want to set with your clientele is that between the tasks you are willing to do and those that you are not willing to do.

Examples:

- Do your clients expect you to help them declutter their house before putting it on the market?

- Do you ever need to tidy up the kitchen of a property before a showing or an open house?

- Do out-of-town sellers often ask you to supervise repairs that they are unable to oversee?

There is a great difference between providing input and referrals for clients and actually taking on the tasks yourself.

NO

Ken: As Realtors® we need to value our time. Occasionally some clients might take advantage and ask us to perform tasks that are unrelated to the transaction. Opening curtains and turning on lights at a property are appropriate tasks; washing dishes in the sink, making beds and watering plants are not.

Jerri: Don't fill your time with tasks that you can delegate or hire out at $15 an hour. It's important to develop the ability to say *"no,"* and, at the same time, provide a solution for your clients.

A suggestion: Provide your clients with a list of recommended individuals and businesses that they can call on for help. This could include names of house cleaners, handymen, contractors, plumbers, gardeners, painters, and professional organizers. Make sure that you vet the names before including them on the list.

Exercise - Setting Task Boundaries

In which areas do you need to set boundaries with your clients? Which tasks do you often take on that are beyond the scope of the real estate transaction?

_____

_____

How will you set task boundaries in the future, while continuing to provide extraordinary service (e.g., delegating the task, referring the client to appropriate resources)?

_____

_____

Key Takeaways

- Set time boundaries with clients, customers, other agents and staff up front so that you are able to take time for yourself.

- Set task boundaries as well. Provide a list of resources to your clients so that you are not personally taking on tasks that are beyond the scope of the real estate transaction.

Key 4: Become Great at Delegating

> **"We all have our certain strengths and we all have our certain weaknesses. The goal is not to fix your weaknesses. The goal is to amplify your strengths and surround yourself with the people who can do what you can't do."**
> – Simon Sinek, author, speaker and leadership consultant

- <u>Neil Lyon</u> is a broker at a large agency in Santa Fe. For the past fifteen years he has been a top-producing agent in his market, including being number one in Santa Fe for many of those years. Neil leads a team of four (all licensed), including an agent-partner, an operations manager, and his wife Cindy, who works part-time.

Neil is an avid mountain biker and skier. He rides several 100 mile road races each summer which *"keep my focus on training"* and heliskis with friends in the West each year.

"<u>Having a team is my vehicle for having a life</u>. I work my tail off when I work. When I play, I play as hard as I work. Having balance in my life has been important to me since 2003, when I had an epiphany: I realized I needed to get control of my life. Every broker who's working 60, 70, or 80 hours a week pines for freedom and free time. As I got older it became obvious that this workstyle wasn't sustainable; I needed to make changes.

"It was then that I realized I needed to grow a team, focused on quality, so that I would be able to have a life. And I took this task seriously. That became my number one priority. To the degree that I have a highly competent team, my business and my clients thrive."

Ken: For many agents, learning to delegate is a huge challenge. They tell me, *"I don't trust anyone to handle my business. How can I go away? Only I can do this."* If you never learn to delegate, you will be on the fast-track for burnout. If you never learn to delegate, you will never have time to go out and create relationships to build your business. And you will never have time to have a life outside of work.

There are four other reasons to become great at delegating:

- You can't do everything by yourself. As your business grows, it will become practically impossible to manage all aspects of your pending transactions while juggling showings and listing presentations, preparing CMAs, following up on new leads and working on the action steps of your business and marketing plan.

- You can't do everything <u>well</u> by yourself. It's not possible to be great at all aspects of your business. As previously stated, top brokers spend their time marketing themselves, obtaining listings, selectively working with buyers, negotiating offers and resolving problems. They hire assistants to manage the details of their transactions. They also hire people to design marketing materials, stage and photograph properties, organize events, update their database, and pay their bills.

**Do the things you are best at, and hire
people to do the things they are best at.**

- It is not cost-effective for you to do everything yourself. Your time is most likely worth between $50 and $400 an hour. You can pay someone else between $15 and $40 an hour to perform many tasks for you. The time you save by delegating can then be spent developing new business and nurturing and expanding your sphere of influence.

- You are empowering others when you delegate aspects of your business. You will derive great satisfaction from seeing people use their creativity, develop their potential, and grow under your management.

<u>How to learn to delegate</u>: If you have an assistant, ask him/her what other tasks they could be doing for you. <u>Then let them do them!</u> If you don't have an assistant, hire temporary help during peak times to assist you with administrative and other non-licensed tasks (such as smoke detector inspections and running errands). Develop reciprocal backup arrangements with other agents in your office for showings and open houses, as needed.

Hire individuals and professional services to do tasks for you in your personal life as well. Hire a cleaning person; use an online food delivery service; hire an image consultant to help you update your wardrobe, if needed. There are a number of people and professional services available to take on jobs and projects that you don't have the time, the interest, or the talent to do. Remember: <u>Play to your strengths</u>, do the things you are best at, and delegate the rest.

A suggestion: Begin with the easiest tasks, and choose someone with whom you enjoy working to help you. Give him or her clear instructions, focusing on the results you want. Be sure to give useful feedback. After you have had some initial success delegating, it will become easier to delegate more important and more complex tasks.

Working With a Virtual Assistant (VA)

There is a relatively new profession of people who work remotely as assistants, many to Realtors ®. Virtual assistants are independent contractors. They are usually paid by the hour, although you can often pay for a bundle of services on a monthly basis. VAs can take on many tasks that do not require a license, including

- marketing (preparing presentations, writing copy and so forth)
- social media management (posting, blogging, updating)
- lead management
- listing coordination

- website design and maintenance

- database management

- bookkeeping

- scheduling and calendar management

- email management, and

- research.

A number of individuals and virtual assistant companies advertise on the internet. Be aware that there are no licensing requirements or standards for virtual assistants, and their training can range from none to certification from an established VA training program. Fees can range from $8 an hour for a VA working overseas to $50 an hour or more for a U.S.-based assistant with specialized training and experience.

The best way to find a VA is through word of mouth. Also worth exploring is Assist U (AssistU.com), a two decades-old VA training company that offers a referral program.

Additional points to note:

- Your VA needs to be trained in your policies, procedures and other ways of doing business.

- You need to be in daily contact with your assistant, so that nothing falls through the cracks, and you can receive updates on tasks and projects and provide instructions and feedback.

- Make sure that your VA signs emails and responds to queries as your assistant, not as you.

- Check with your manager and with your local real estate board to make sure you are in compliance with your company's policies as well as with real estate laws and regulations in your state.

Growing Beyond the Solo Agent Model

As you become more successful, you may want to hire staff and grow a team. Or you may want to partner with another agent. We suggest that you grow your business in an "organic" way, hiring staff and expending resources as your business grows and as your budget and cash flow allow.

A typical growth pattern for a solo agent is:

- First, enlist temporary help on an "as needed" basis, with backup arrangements in place with a licensed agent so that you can take time off.
- Next, hire an assistant who is a licensed agent who can provide backup, perform showings, write offers, and so on, as well as perform administrative duties. (A general rule of thumb is to have one assistant for every 40 or 50 transactions per year.)
- Then, get a full-time buyer's agent.
- Finally, develop a team, with an assistant, a transaction manager, buyer's agents, listing agents, and marketing support (including, perhaps, a social media manager). The configuration is obviously up to you, and will depend upon your market and your goals, especially how big you want to grow your business.

In Appendix A we offer four models for operating a successful real estate business, ranging from the solo agent to a partnership to a team.

Exercise - Getting Great at Delegating

In the space below, list three tasks you are willing to delegate right now, and to whom you will delegate them (for example, to a part-time assistant, an administrator in your office or to a graphic designer).

Task   To Whom I Will Delegate

1.

2.

3.

Extra credit: List one task you *know* you should delegate, but aren't willing to right now, and choose a date by which you will delegate this task.

Task   Date

1.

Key Takeaways

- Learning to delegate is key to having a life.
- Do the things you are best at, and hire people to do the things they are best at.
- Use part time assistants, virtual assistants, and professional services to delegate tasks without hiring full time staff.
- Delegation is a process: begin with the easiest tasks first.
- There are various models for growing a team or creating a partnership with another agent.

Key 5: Take Great Care of Yourself

"Sleep is the best meditation."
– Dalai Lama

"I've learned that when we care for ourselves deeply and deliberately, we naturally begin to care for others...in a healthier and more effective way."
– Cheryl Richardson, author and life coach

So-called "extreme self-care" is a major concept in coaching. The idea is to make the quality of your own life your top priority. Take as good care of yourself as you do of your clients, partner, children and pets.

This is a <u>radical concept</u> in a business in which agents bend over backwards for their clients, losing sleep, missing family dinners, shortening vacations, and so forth in the name of the deal.

We're not suggesting that you stop giving extraordinary service to your clients and customers; just that you not lose sight of what else is important to you.

Good health is a cornerstone of extreme self-care.

Eating well, eating "clean" (unprocessed and organic foods), limiting alcohol, caffeine, sugar and white flour, and exercising regularly will keep you healthy and give you more energy. Massages, meditation and other relaxation techniques will be restorative.

Find a way to de-stress, whether by practicing yoga, power-walking, deep breathing, or taking baths. All are great ways of taking time from business and focusing <u>on you</u>. Actually sit down and eat lunch.

Perhaps the most important point: GET ENOUGH SLEEP. Too often we don't realize that our body requires a certain amount of sleep. If we fail to heed it we pay the price in lack of energy, increased mistakes, irritability, and decreased focus. Make a point of going to bed <u>one hour earlier</u> each night for a week and see if you notice a difference. Also, refrain from drinking caffeinated beverages after 2 pm.

A Sleep Ritual

- One hour before going to bed, put your smartphone on silent mode, preferably in another room. (You can program your Iphone to let designated callers ring through even if the phone is silenced.) This will ensure that you won't be disturbed unless there is an emergency.

- Turn off the television or turn off loud music. Put your laptop or tablet away.

- Electronic devices emit blue light which has been shown to inhibit the production of melatonin and thus interfere with high-quality sleep. (If you must use a computer or e-reader before bed, you can purchase blue-light blocking glasses online for less than ten dollars or you can download a color-shifting app called f.lux.)

- Make sure your bedroom is cool. According to the National Sleep Foundation, *"the suggested bedroom temperature should be between 60 and 67 degrees Fahrenheit for optimal sleep."*

- Turn down the lights 30 minutes before getting into bed. Now is a perfect time to meditate or listen to soft, relaxing music. If you put a few drops of lavender oil on your pillow or on a hand towel it will help you relax even further.

- Turn off the lights (make sure the room is dark) and have a good night's sleep.

Another great way to take care of yourself is to <u>take time off</u>. This is <u>critical</u>, and difficult for many agents who are afraid of losing business. But taking days off and taking vacations are essential for your well-being, and for the health of your relationships and family life. When you are burnt out, tired and frustrated, what kind of energy are you sending out?

Here are stories from two very different top producers who have successfully integrated self-care into their busy lives:

- Gail Roberts has been the number one broker in Cambridge, Massachusetts for the past ten years. Cambridge is home to Harvard University and MIT, and is a highly educated luxury real estate market. Gail leads a team of five. Here are some of her secrets for taking great care of herself while running a very successful business:

  "I try to get up at the same time every day. I have breakfast, check emails and then spend between 45 and 60 minutes on the elliptical machine at home. My trainer comes twice a week to my house. It's an appointment that I make sure I keep.

  "I also make sure that I take time for lunch. When I go to lunch I need to disconnect from the phone. It's important to sit down, take time to connect in person with colleagues, clients or friends and not be constantly watching the phone or texting.

  "I don't generally work from home. When I get home from the office I like to unwind and decompress. I do check emails in the evening and before I go to bed. I try to get between seven and eight hours of sleep every night. Sleep is so important.

  "And I go to a health and wellness spa in Western Mass. every couple of months for four or five days—for as much time as I can. I find the early morning walks, meditations and massages really recharge me."

- Neil Lyon, the Santa Fe broker quoted earlier, integrates exercise and personal time into his schedule in a different way:

  "I get up early and work out starting at 5:45 or 6:00 am five mornings a week. I have breakfast and then work at home answering emails from 7:30 to 8:30 or 9:00 am.

"I go to the office or to showings and work until noon or so, when I have a quick lunch, usually at my desk. A nice benefit of working with my wife Cindy is that I get to see her several times a day when I'm working. I usually work until 5:30 or 6:00 pm.

"I put biking on my calendar. Two or three days a week I bike before dinner, indoors in the winter, and outside on the riding trails for one and a half or two and a half hours once it's daylight saving time.

"I have dinner with Cindy every night. Then, for 30 minutes after dinner I answer emails or do work requiring quiet time.

"I'm in a really good place sleep-wise. I get seven hours of sleep a night."

Notice how each of these brokers has deliberately designed her/his schedule to incorporate exercise, sufficient sleep, time with family and friends, and days off into a busy life.

One of their secrets is developing <u>rituals</u>—*"detailed method(s) or procedure(s) faithfully or regularly followed"*—and <u>habits</u>—*"recurrent, often unconscious pattern(s) of behavior that (are) acquired through frequent repetition"*—that they maintain without fail. (Definitions are from *The American Heritage Dictionary*.) These rituals and habits become ingrained as part of their lives, as routine as brushing their teeth or checking their emails.

Ken: Everyone who is at the top of their field—whether an athlete, musician, actor or real estate agent—has rituals that he or she follows. Top performing agents have rituals such as going to yoga class each morning, making ten phone calls to leads daily, having standing planning appointments with themselves weekly, and having coffee with a client or referral partner each week.

Jerri: What self-care and other rituals can you do on a daily or weekly basis to ensure your good health and the good health of your business?

Exercise - Taking Time for Yourself

- Take out your calendar and schedule at least <u>one week off</u> in the next six months. (*We give you permission!*) Figure out how you will get backup coverage (with a team member, another agent in your office, or someone else). You might want to schedule vacations around holidays when business might be slower.

- Also schedule a <u>half-day or day off</u> within the next two weeks and again, decide how you will get coverage.

- Finally, make dinner plans with family or friends <u>at least one</u> night this week, so that you won't be working until 9 or 10 pm.

Remember, having backup coverage is key to actually taking time off.

Jerri: I once had a client who went on a weeklong Caribbean cruise. When she returned she remarked that she had rung up $800 in cell phone charges talking to clients and customers. What kind of vacation could she possibly have had while being on the phone for most of the time?

A great resource for learning more about self-care is Cheryl Richardson's book, *The Art of Extreme Self-Care: Transform Your Life One Month at a Time.*

Exercise - Taking Care of Yourself

1. What are <u>five</u> things that you can do on a daily basis to help keep you physically, mentally, emotionally and spiritually well? (*Examples: eat a salad every day; take vitamin supplements; meditate for at least ten minutes in the morning.*) List them below and also on page 156 of the Blueprint.

1.

2.

3.

4.

5.

2. What's <u>one change</u> you can make that will have a <u>major impact</u> upon the quality of your life this month? *(It might be taking Friday afternoons off from work, giving up caffeine, or taking salsa or tango lessons.)*

3. What's something that you can <u>remove</u> from your life that will make a big difference? *(It could be spending too much time on social media, buying things you don't really need, or putting up with difficult clients.)*

<u>Key Takeaways</u>

- Make self-care, especially your own good health, a top priority.
- Eat well, manage stress and get enough sleep.
- Take time off!

Key 6: Give Back

"From what we get, we can make a living. What we give, however, makes a life."
– Tennis great Arthur Ashe

"Only a life lived for others is a life worthwhile."
– Albert Einstein

There are many ways of giving back to the community which has given to you; it's not just about donating money.

> **Jerri:** Many years ago I was working with a terrific agent who told me, *"I make a ridiculous amount of money and don't need to think about how to make more. Instead, I'd like to find a meaningful volunteer activity. I don't know exactly what that is, but sometimes I get tired of being the staid financial advisor. Now and then, if I want to wake up with green hair, I should be able to do that."* He also said that he wanted to put balance in his life by focusing on other pieces of himself that he had ignored.
>
> I happened to know a woman who was starting a clown troupe that performed at local children's hospitals, and voilà, more than fifteen years later, <u>Alan Cohen</u>, senior sales associate at a firm in Brookline, Massachusetts, is still volunteering with the Hearts & Noses Hospital Clown Troupe as a hospital troupe clown, performing at Boston Medical Center and Floating Hospital for Children.

Giving back is key to both happiness and success.

The joy of giving for the sake of giving cannot be overstated. When you give of yourself, you join a community of like-minded people which offers a level of connection and satisfaction not often found as readily in the work domain.

There are countless ways to give back, including

- Donating a percentage or fixed dollar amount of each commission to a favorite nonprofit or a charitable gift fund;
- Serving on the board of directors of a local hospital;
- Volunteering your time for service projects (such as painting a homeless shelter or collecting food and financial donations for a food bank);
- Biking or running for a charity event; or
- Organizing a silent auction for a fundraiser.

As Coach Thomas Leonard once said, *"Add value just for the joy of it."* You will have fun and derive great satisfaction if you choose ways to give back that are meaningful to you. And it may even help you attract more business.

Exercise - Giving Back

How will you give back to your community? List one way in which you will give back (if you are not doing so already) and the date by which you will begin in the space below.

1.   <u>Date</u>

Key Takeaways

- Giving back is key to both happiness and success.
- There are countless ways to give back. Find a way that resonates with you.
- Give for the joy of giving, expecting nothing in return.

Key 7: Express Gratefulness

> **"When I started counting my blessings, my whole life turned around."**
> – Singer Willie Nelson

> **"The only prayer you ever need is 'Thank You.'"**
> – Theologian Meister Eckhart

You are now well on your way to creating the business and the life that you desire. The final step is to express appreciation for all that you have and all that you are creating.

Expressing gratitude is about acknowledging and being thankful for everything that you have in your life.

Author Deepak Chopra has said that expressing gratefulness *"opens the door"* to creating more abundance. Even if you wake up with a headache and in a foul mood, by expressing gratitude for your breath, for your comfortable bed, for the possibilities awaiting you in the day ahead, you can turn your day around and attract positive energy.

Many people have written about the value of keeping a gratitude list or journal, in which you write down three things for which you are grateful every night. (Author Sheryl Sandberg calls these *"moments of joy."*) This is a terrific exercise. Another is one in which you and your family go around the dinner table each evening and tell each other several things for which you are grateful. Acknowledging the blessings in your life produces momentum for creating even more of what you want.

- <u>Jeremy Bowers</u> is the manager of a large agency in Philadelphia, PA. Jeremy grew up in the town of Punxsutawney, PA where his dad was a pharmacist. As a kid, Jeremy attended many patients' funerals with his father, and heard a number of eulogies. *"I realized that most people don't tell others what they appreciate about them when they are alive. When you feel it, you should be saying it."*

Jeremy resolved to tell people what he appreciated about them in the moment, instead of waiting until it was too late.

"I tell three people a day what I appreciate about them. I call everyone who does a deal with my agency and thank them. And I write two or three thank you cards every day or send a book or a gift to people. I also journal on a daily basis, writing down four or five things I'm thankful for.

"I've moved up the ranks by telling people what I appreciate about them. It's also created a climate of positivity in my office."

Exercise - Expressing Gratefulness

Each evening, for the next seven days, write down three things for which you are grateful. You can either use the spaces below, or use a separate gratitude list or journal. (You can even keep a list in the Notes section of your smartphone.) Notice how you feel as you are writing the items down, and notice the impact this exercise is beginning to have on your life.

Day one:

1.

2.

3.

Day two:

1.

2.

3.

Day three:

1.

2.

3.

Day four:

1.

2.

3.

Day five:

1.

2.

3.

Day six:

1.

2.

3.

Day seven:

1.

2.

3.

Key Takeaways

- Expressing gratitude is about acknowledging and appreciating everything that you have in your life.

- Gratitude is the final step in the creation process. It brings more joy and positivity to your life and to the lives of those you touch.

Conclusion

You have been reading this book and completing the exercises for some time now. Here is an opportunity to go back to your initial goals and review the results that you have created so far. Notice the steps you have taken, acknowledge your progress, and decide what new or different actions you want to take to help you move <u>even further ahead</u>.

This is a chance to reflect and to celebrate.

Take your time, answer the questions below, and <u>really think about the steps you've taken, the progress you've made, and the results you've created since you started this book</u>. Then allow the impact of what you've done to really sink in. It's okay—even great—to smile and feel good about yourself!

Exercise - Reflections and Summation

Write down three results you've produced and/or three changes that you've made in your business or in your life since you started working with this book:

1.

2.

3.

Write down three insights that you've gained about yourself and your business:

1.

2.

3.

Review your initial business goals on page 19, and either modify them or replace them with new goals below:

1.

2.

3.

4.

5.

Review your life goals on pages 94-95 and either modify them or create new goals for yourself:

1.

2.

3.

You have now created a blueprint for the next twelve months. Read your goals frequently, visualize yourself having achieved them, and update them as they manifest!

Great Work!

Extra credit: write three goals to achieve within the next three years:

1.

2.

3.

Within the next five years:

1.

2.

3.

<u>Congratulations</u>! Thank you for having taken the time to challenge yourself, to examine the ways that you have been conducting your business and living your life, and to discover new ways of being and working. And thank you for your commitment to your personal growth and to the growth of your business.

If you've been fully engaged in this process, you are now on your way to becoming even more successful and having a life you love.

u have learned a number of tips, techniques and strategies to help you ecome clear about what you want and to enable you to move forward and achieve your goals. Just as musicians, dancers and painters practice their craft, you need to practice the principles presented in this book.

We recommend that you go back and review the material <u>at least once a year</u>. As you and your business grow and evolve, so too will your goals.

We would love to hear about your successes and your experience with this book. You can email us at info@tremontpress.com.

Join our Facebook group, <u>Beyond the Sale—for Real Estate Agents,</u> where you can connect with other agents (and us) to ask and answer questions on topics in this book. It is also a place for you to get support from us and from other agents throughout the country.

Subscribe to our email list for free updates, tips and workshop information. Send an email with "Subscribe me" in the subject line to info@TremontPress.com.

- If you want to learn more about real estate coaching or about business coaching, either for yourself or for your team, contact Jerri at Jerri@tremontpress.com.
- If you want to learn more about working as a Coldwell Banker agent, contact Ken at Ken@tremontpress.com.
- If you want to find out about presentations, workshops and seminars with the authors, contact us at info@tremontpress.com.

We wish you tremendous success!

© Jerri N. Udelson and Ken Tutunjian, 2018

Blueprint for Success

Note: Please don't fill out this Blueprint until you've actually completed the exercises in the book. Your responses below are derived from the work you've done since beginning this process. They reflect your thoughtful and honest answers to the questions we've posed throughout.

Three copies of the Blueprint are included here so that you can update or revise your goals and action steps as desired.

Date _____

List your top three values (from page 12) below:

1.

2.

3.

What is your purpose in being in real estate (what motivates you) (from page 14)?

What are your top ten strengths (from pages 32-33)? Include a brief description of each strength *(e.g., Activator® - turning thoughts into action)*.

1.

2.

3.

4.

5.

6.

7.

8.

9.

10.

List your top five business goals (from page 19) for the coming twelve months.

1.

2.

3.

4.

5.

Using these goals as a basis, write down three <u>non-marketing business objectives</u> (from pages 68-69) that you want to implement <u>within the</u> next six months.

Then, for each objective list the <u>action steps</u> required to carry out that objective and the <u>date</u> by which you will have taken each step. Put each deadline on your calendar.

Objective 1. _____

Action Steps:	Action Step Deadlines:
1.	_____
2.	_____
3.	_____
4.	_____
5.	_____

Objective 2. _____

        Action Steps: Action Step Deadlines:

1.   _____

2.   _____

3.   _____

4.   _____

5.   _____

Objective 3. _____

        Action Steps: Action Step Deadlines:

1.   _____

2.   _____

3.   _____

4.   _____

5.   _____

List three <u>long-term marketing strategies</u> (from pages 72-73) that you want to implement. For each strategy <u>list the action steps</u> required to carry out the strategy and <u>the date</u> by which you will have taken each step. Put each deadline on your calendar.

Strategy A. _____

              Action Steps: Action Step Deadlines:

1. _____ _____

2. _____ _____

3. _____ _____

4. _____ _____

5. _____ _____

Strategy B. _____

              Action Steps: Action Step Deadlines:

1. _____ _____

2. _____ _____

3. _____ _____

4. _____ _____

5. _____ _____

Strategy C. _____

          Action Steps: Action Step Deadlines:

1.   _____

2.   _____

3.   _____

4.   _____

5.   _____

For each of the following categories, rate your level of satisfaction on a scale of 1 to 10, 1 being "completely unsatisfied" and 10 being "completely satisfied." (This exercise is from pages 93-94.)

Significant other/romance   _____

Friends and family   _____

Health   _____

Home environment   _____

Fun, play and recreation   _____

Creative expression   _____

Personal growth   _____

Other _____   _____

Choose three categories on which you want to focus. They could be categories with the lowest ratings or categories that appeal to you the most. Create a goal for each of these categories, writing your goals in the positive, and specifying deadlines, if appropriate. (This exercise is from pages 96-99.)

Write three life goals with accompanying action steps and deadlines in the spaces below:

Goal 1: _____

	Action Steps:	Action Step Deadlines:
1.		_____
2.		_____
3.		_____
4.		_____
5.		_____

Goal 2: _____

	Action Steps:	Action Step Deadlines:
1.		_____
2.		_____
3.		_____
4.		_____
5.		_____

Goal 3: _____

Action Steps: Action Step Deadlines:

1.   _____

2.   _____

3.   _____

4.   _____

5.   _____

Make sure to put each deadline on your calendar.

List five things that you can do on a daily basis to help keep you physically, mentally, emotionally and spiritually well (from page 135). *(Examples: eat a salad every day; take vitamin supplements; meditate for at least ten minutes each morning.)*

1.

2.

3.

4.

5.

Blueprint for Success

Date _____

List your top three values (from page 12) below:

1.

2.

3.

What is your purpose in being in real estate (what motivates you) (from page 14)?

What are your top ten strengths (from pages 32-33)? Include a brief description of each strength *(e.g., Activator® - turning thoughts into action)*.

1.

2.

3.

4.

5.

6.

7.

8.

9.

10.

List your top five business goals (from page 19) for the coming twelve months.

1.

2.

3.

4.

5.

Using these goals as a basis, write down three <u>non-marketing business objectives</u> (from pages 68-69) that you want to implement <u>within the</u> next six months.

Then, for each objective list the <u>action steps</u> required to carry out that objective and the <u>date</u> by which you will have taken each step. Put each deadline on your calendar.

Objective 1. _____

             Action Steps: Action Step Deadlines:

1. _____

2. _____

3. _____

4. _____

5. _____

Objective 2. _____

        Action Steps: Action Step Deadlines:

1.   _____

2.   _____

3.   _____

4.   _____

5.   _____

Objective 3. _____

        Action Steps: Action Step Deadlines:

1.   _____

2.   _____

3.   _____

4.   _____

5.   _____

List three <u>long-term marketing strategies</u> (from pages 72-73) that you want to implement. For each strategy <u>list the action steps</u> required to carry out the strategy and <u>the date</u> by which you will have taken each step. Put each deadline on your calendar.

Strategy A._____

           Action Steps: Action Step Deadlines:

   1.   _____

   2.   _____

   3.   _____

   4.   _____

   5.   _____

Strategy B. _____

           Action Steps: Action Step Deadlines:

   1.   _____

   2.   _____

   3.   _____

   4.   _____

   5.   _____

Strategy C. _____

                Action Steps: Action Step Deadlines:

1.   _____

2.   _____

3.   _____

4.   _____

5.   _____

For each of the following categories, rate your level of satisfaction on a scale of 1 to 10, 1 being "completely unsatisfied" and 10 being "completely satisfied." (This exercise is from pages 93-94.)

Significant other/romance   _____

Friends and family   _____

Health   _____

Home environment   _____

Fun, play and recreation   _____

Creative expression   _____

Personal growth   _____

Other _____   _____

Choose three categories on which you want to focus. They could be categories with the lowest ratings or categories that appeal to you the most. Create a goal for each of these categories, writing your goals in the positive, and specifying deadlines, if appropriate. (This exercise is from pages 96-99.)

Write three life goals with accompanying action steps and deadlines in the spaces below:

Goal 1: _____

                    Action Steps: Action Step Deadlines:

1.   _____

2.   _____

3.   _____

4.   _____

5.   _____

Goal 2: _____

                    Action Steps: Action Step Deadlines:

1.   _____

2.   _____

3.   _____

4.   _____

5.   _____

Goal 3: _____

Action Steps: Action Step Deadlines:

    1.   _____

    2.   _____

    3.   _____

    4.   _____

    5.   _____

Make sure to put each deadline on your calendar.

List five things that you can do on a daily basis to help keep you physically, mentally, emotionally and spiritually well (from page 135). *(Examples: eat a salad every day; take vitamin supplements; meditate for at least ten minutes each morning.)*

1.

2.

3.

4.

5.

Blueprint for Success

Date _____

List your top three values (from page 12) below:

1.

2.

3.

What is your purpose in being in real estate (what motivates you) (from page 14)?

What are your top ten strengths (from pages 32-33)? Include a brief description of each strength *(e.g., Activator® - turning thoughts into action)*.

1.

2.

3.

4.

5.

6.

7.

8.

9.

10.

List your top five business goals (from page 19) for the coming twelve months.

1.

2.

3.

4.

5.

Using these goals as a basis, write down three <u>non-marketing business objectives</u> (from pages 68-69) that you want to implement <u>within the next six months</u>.

Then, for each objective list the <u>action steps</u> required to carry out that objective and the <u>date</u> by which you will have taken each step. Put each deadline on your calendar.

Objective 1. _____

Action Steps: Action Step Deadlines:

1.   _____

2.   _____

3.   _____

4.   _____

5.   _____

Objective 2. _____

           Action Steps: Action Step Deadlines:

1. _____

2. _____

3. _____

4. _____

5. _____

Objective 3. _____

           Action Steps: Action Step Deadlines:

1. _____

2. _____

3. _____

4. _____

5. _____

List three <u>long-term marketing strategies</u> (from pages 72-73) that you want to implement. For each strategy <u>list the action steps</u> required to carry out the strategy and <u>the date</u> by which you will have taken each step. Put each deadline on your calendar.

Strategy A._____

             Action Steps: Action Step Deadlines:

1.   _____

2.   _____

3.   _____

4.   _____

5.   _____

Strategy B. _____

             Action Steps: Action Step Deadlines:

1.   _____

2.   _____

3.   _____

4.   _____

5.   _____

Strategy C. _____

                 Action Steps: Action Step Deadlines:

1.   _____

2.   _____

3.   _____

4.   _____

5.   _____

For each of the following categories, rate your level of satisfaction on a scale of 1 to 10, 1 being "completely unsatisfied" and 10 being "completely satisfied." (This exercise is from pages 93-94.)

Significant other/romance   _____

Friends and family   _____

Health   _____

Home environment   _____

Fun, play and recreation   _____

Creative expression   _____

Personal growth   _____

Other _____   _____

Choose three categories on which you want to focus. They could be categories with the lowest ratings or categories that appeal to you the most. Create a goal for each of these categories, writing your goals in the positive, and specifying deadlines, if appropriate. (This exercise is from pages 96-99.)

Write three life goals with accompanying action steps and deadlines in the spaces below:

Goal 1: _____

                     Action Steps: **Action Step Deadlines:**

1.   _____

2.   _____

3.   _____

4.   _____

5.   _____

Goal 2: _____

                     Action Steps: **Action Step Deadlines:**

1.   _____

2.   _____

3.   _____

4.   _____

5.   _____

Goal 3: _____

Action Steps:	Action Step Deadlines:
1.	_____
2.	_____
3.	_____
4.	_____
5.	_____

Make sure to put each deadline on your calendar.

List five things that you can do on a daily basis to help keep you physically, mentally, emotionally and spiritually well (from page 135). *(Examples: eat a salad every day; take vitamin supplements; meditate for at least ten minutes each morning.)*

1.

2.

3.

4.

5.

APPENDIX A

<u>Models for Operating a Successful Real Estate Business</u>

There are various models for operating a successful real estate business.

Among the most common are:
- Solo agent with reciprocal backup
- Solo agent with paid backup
- Partnership
- Team.

Note that these four models are <u>operating models</u> and <u>not legal forms of business organization</u> such as C corporations, S corporations, LLCs, partnerships and sole proprietorships. For more information on legal structures for your business, consult your attorney and your accountant.

- <u>In the solo agent with reciprocal backup model</u> an agent pairs with a like-minded officemate, and each covers for the other so they can take time off as well as vacation time. This is an informal agreement, and not necessarily ongoing. The financial arrangements between agents are worked out ahead of time, specifying commission splits when the covering agent makes a sale or lists a property.

- In the solo agent with paid backup model an agent pays other agents for backup, as needed, most likely on an hourly and commission basis. In this model, agents can get support from several agents and licensed assistants. When you are busy or want to take time off, it makes sense to have other agents cover your business, including open houses, home inspections and showings. Again, the financial arrangements need to be specified in advance.

- In the partnership model two agents join forces on a 50-50 basis to support one another's business. Neither one reports to the other. Partners cover for one another. They may go on listing presentations together, and they generally share buyers and listings. If it turns out that one of the partners is truly a rainmaker– bringing in most of the business–while the other partner excels at overseeing and running the operation, then the partners may decide to change the financial arrangement to reflect the greater value that the rainmaker brings to the table. Or the partnership may morph into a team.

- In the team model there is a leader, deemed the president, CEO, or managing broker. There is a clear division of tasks and roles, with the job of the team members to support the team leader. Typically, there are administrative support staff (e.g., an executive assistant and/or transaction manager), buyer's agents, listing agents, marketing support, and perhaps a social media manager. The team usually operates under the leader's name, and members are paid under various arrangements (including salaries for the assistant(s) and commissions and perhaps a share of the profits for other team members).

If one of the team members develops into a rainmaker, bringing substantial business to the team, then the team can transition into a partnership, with that member taking on an executive role, and the other team members reporting to a designated partner.

Sometimes two agents pair up as a partnership within someone else's team. Sometimes two partners within a team hire administrative support and find a buyer's agent to work with them. <u>No one model works for everyone</u>. And one model can morph into another as your business grows and your needs, interests, and goals change.

If you are planning to exit the real estate business at some point, nurturing a rainmaker on the team or in the partnership is a good way to begin to transition out of the business. This could be the first step in an <u>exit strategy</u> that will allow you to turn over your book of business to someone who will provide a stream of income to you after you retire.

Ken: Emily came into my office sobbing. She was supposed to partner with John, but she couldn't do it. She couldn't give up control to someone else, someone she considered a very good friend as well as someone she enjoyed working with. I said, *"You don't have to do it. Don't turn yourself inside out."*

She kept wailing and became very dramatic. Emily and John did not become partners. Emily had a brilliant career, always working solo. She didn't need to work with anyone. When she wanted to take time off, she paid an officemate for backup.

Jerri: Partnerships and teams are not for everyone. A lot of people go into real estate because they want to be independent entrepreneurs. They want to be in control. As they become more successful and grow a team, they often find that they have become what I call "reluctant managers." This doesn't necessarily work. If you find yourself in this situation, the right move might be to scale back.

APPENDIX B

<u>List of Exercises</u>

Exercise	Page Number(s)
What Are Your Top Three Values?	12
What is Your Purpose?	14
Where Are You Right Now?	15-18
Creating Goals for Your Business	18-19
What Are You Telling Yourself?	23-24
What Do You Believe About Yourself?	25-26
Visualizing Your Goals	28-29
Creating a Vision Board	30
Your Top Ten Strengths	32-33
Looking at What's Worked for You	35-37
Where Does Your Business Come From?	38-39
Looking at Fear	48-49
Creating Your Short-Term Business Objectives	66-69
Your Marketing Plan	70-73
Finalizing Your Business and Marketing Plan	75
Your Commitment	83
How Will You Remain Accountable?	86
Creating Life Goals	93-95
Creating an Action Plan for Your Life Goals	96-99
Creating an Intimate Relationship	103-105

The Symbolic Gesture   106
Providing Extraordinary Service   114
Becoming More Organized and Productive   118
Setting Time Boundaries   121
Setting Task Boundaries   123
Getting Great at Delegating   128-129
Taking Time for Yourself   134
Taking Care of Yourself   134-135
Giving Back   137
Expressing Gratefulness   139-141
Reflections and Summation   143-145
Blueprint for Success   149-156

Resources

Introduction

Books

Rath, Tom. *StrengthsFinder® 2.0* New York: Gallup Press, 2007.

Whitworth, et al. *Co-Active Coaching: New Skills for Coaching People Toward Success in Work and Life.* Mountain View, CA: Davies-Black Publishing, 2007.

Websites

gallupstrengthscenter.com. Purchase the Strengthsfinder® - All 34 Strengths Access and the *StrengthsFinder® 2.0* e-book online.

Part I: Creating a Great Business

Books

Duckworth, Angela. *Grit: The Power of Passion and Perseverance.* New York: Scribner, 2016.

Fritz, Robert. *The Path of Least Resistance: Learning to Become the Creative Force in Your Own Life.* New York: Random House, 1989.

Helmstetter, Shad. *What to Say When You Talk to Your Self.* New York: Simon & Schuster, 2017.

Helmstetter, Shad. *365 Days of Positive Self-Talk.* Gulf Breeze, FL: Park Avenue Press, 2015.

Jeffers, Susan. *Feel the Fear and Do It Anyway.* New York: Random House, 2006.

ance, Katie. *#GetSocialSmart: How to Hone Your Social Media Strategy.* elf-published, 2017.

Richardson, Cheryl. *Stand Up for Your Life.* New York: Simon & Schuster, 2002.

Rubin, Gretchen. *The Four Tendencies: The Indispensable Personality Profiles That Reveal How to Make Your Life Better (and Other People's Lives Better, Too).* New York: Penguin Random House, 2017.

Rubin, Gretchen. *Better Than Before: Mastering the Habits of Our Everyday Lives.* New York: Crown Publishers, 2015.

Websites

archagent.com (select PowerDialer) - dialing system for prospecting

dwell.com - a good source of articles to repost online

espressoagent.com - lead generation system and CRM manager

federalreserve.gov/boarddocs/supmanual/cch/respa.pdf - Real Estate Settlement Procedures Act (RESPA) of 1974

getrileynow.com - custom concierge service for 24/7 lead follow up

gretchenrubin.com - You can take the Four Tendencies Quiz. (How you respond to expectations)

inman.com - good source of articles to repost

katielance.com - social media strategist and consultant

meetup.com - to find a local group of people who share your interests

mikeferry.com/main/content/complimentary - You can get free scripts for real estate agents.

mojosells.com Mojo dialing - lead manager and dialing systems

nar.realtor/code-of-ethics

rokrbox.com - lead conversion process

theredx.com - lead generation, management and prospecting system

vulcan7.com - lead generation system

website designers: WIX.com, RealEstateDesigner.com, RealtyTech.com, AgentImage.com, RealEstateWebmasters.com, RockhopperMediaGroup.com, BoomtownRoi.com

youtube.com - Simon Sinek's Top Ten Rules for Success

Ted Talks (ted.com)

Simon Sinek - How good leaders inspire action

Facebook Group

Beyond the Sale—for Real Estate Agents

Part II: Creating a Life You Love

Books

Leonard, Thomas J. *The Portable Coach: 28 Surefire Strategies for Business and Personal Success.* New York: Scribner, 1998.

Rubin, Gretchen. *The Happiness Project.* New York: HarperCollins, 2009.

Stoltzfus, Tony. *Coaching Questions: A Coach's Guide to Powerful Asking Skills.* Self-published, 2008.

Podcasts

Happier with Gretchen Rubin
The James Altucher Show
The Minimalists Podcasts

Ted Talks (ted.com)

Brené Brown - The power of vulnerability

Part III: Tips from Top Producers: Seven Keys to Success

Books

Bailey, Chris. *The Productivity Project: Accomplishing More by Managing Your Time, Attention, and Energy Better.* New York: Crown Business, 2016.

Gawande, Atul. *The Checklist Manifesto: How to Get Things Right.* New York: Picador, 2010.

Godin, Seth. *Linchpin: Are You Indispensable?* New York: Portfolio/Penguin, 2011.

McKeown, Greg. *Essentialism: The Disciplined Pursuit of Less.* New York: Penguin Random House, 2014.

Richardson, Cheryl. *The Art of Extreme Self-Care: Transform Your Life One Month at a Time.* Carlsbad, CA: Hay House, 2009.

Richardson, Cheryl. *Take Time for Your Life: A Personal Coach's 7-Step Program for Creating the Life You Want.* New York: Broadway Books, 1998.

Sandberg, Sheryl and Grant, Adam. *Option B: Facing Adversity, Building Resilience, and Finding Joy.* New York: Knopf Doubleday, 2017.

Sinek, Simon. *Start with Why: How Great Leaders Inspire Everyone to Take Action.* New York: Penguin Group, 2011.

Tracy, Brian. *Eat That Frog! 21 Great Ways to Stop Procrastinating and Get More Done in Less Time.* San Francisco: Berrett-Koehler Publishers, 2001.

Websites

alifeofproductivity.com - for time management tips and techniques

assistu.com - virtual assistant training and referral company

cherylrichardson.com - sign up for a weekly blog on the topic of self-care

matterport.com - 3D walkthroughs, photos, videos and VR for listings

tinyhabits.com - a free program to create new behaviors in your life

Apps

Moment - screen time tracker

Dormio - to sleep better tonight

F.lux - color shifting app - for use before bed

Headspace - meditation app

Insight Timer - meditation app

Featured Agents

Alexandra Conigliaro Biega, Boston, MA	*www.biegakilgoreteam.com*
Jeremy Bowers, Philadelphia, PA	*www.thejeremybowers.com*
Hans Brings, Waltham, MA	*www.hansbrings.com*
Dustin Brohm, Salt Lake City, UT	*www.searchsaltlake.com*
Wil Catlin, Boston, MA	*www.bostonofficespaces.com*
Alan Cohen, Brookline, Newton, MA	*www.alancohensellshomes.com*
Margot Rose Edde, San Francisco	*www.climbsf.com*
Cindy Lyon, Santa Fe, NM	*www.neillyon.com*
Neil Lyon, Santa Fe, NM	*www.neillyon.com*
Janet Reilly, Carmel, CA	*www.sothebyshomes.com*
Gail Roberts, Cambridge, MA	*www.gailroberts.com*
Ben Snow, Boston, MA	*www.bensnowre.com*

Acknowledgments

This book could not have been written without the input of so many wonderful people. Thanks to our early readers, Ann Roosevelt, Cindy Lyon, Dara Kosberg, Johanna Omelia, Hans Brings, David Goldsmith, Linda Huizenga, Tom Udelson, and Jeff Kosberg. A special thanks to Marcia Polese for her invaluable suggestions and feedback.

We are grateful for the contributions of many agents and others who have added to the narrative: Thalia Tringo, Wil Catlin, Margot Rose Edde, Neil Lyon, Jeremy Bowers, Stephen Burdick, Gail Roberts, Paul Whaley, Kyle Elizabeth, Katie Lance, Alexandra Conigliaro Biega, Alan Cohen, Cindy Lyon, Ben Snow, Dustin Brohm, Janet Reilly, James Rice, Esq., and Peter Mullane, Esq.

To Alex Hanna and Katie Mingo, our extraordinarily talented graphic designers, many thanks.

<u>Jerri</u>: There's a huge amount of gratitude reserved for our wonderful coach and colleague Cheryl Richardson and for the brilliant Robert Fritz. Cheryl, you are a wise soul who has touched so many lives. And Bob, you were the first person to teach me that you can really create what you want. Much appreciation to you both.

<u>Ken</u>: Thank you to all of the people who supported me and helped me create my personal and professional vision, especially Cheryl Richardson, Kathryn Hayward, MD, Laura Gray, Bill Kiley, and Merit McIntyre.

About the Authors

<u>Jerri Udelson</u> has been called a "coaching pioneer and visionary." One of the first one hundred people to be designated a Master Certified Coach by the International Coaching Federation, Jerri is the founder of International Coaching Week, now celebrated worldwide in countries as disparate as Nigeria, India and the United Kingdom.

Her coaching company, Entrepreneurial Coaching and Consulting, focuses on helping real estate agents, entrepreneurs and self-employed professionals grow their businesses quickly and strategically, while also creating lives they love outside of work.

Clients have called her *"direct and insightful," "terrific to work with," "very caring and intuitive,"* and *"warm, fun to talk to, and non-judgmental."*

Jerri has been a licensed real estate broker in Massachusetts for over twenty-five years. Prior to starting her coaching business she was a consultant to startups in Boston and the COO and CFO of a training company.

Jerri lives in Santa Fe, NM with her partner and their Siamese cats. She coaches worldwide, via phone, text and email.

<u>Ken Tutunjian</u> has been the vice president and manager of two Coldwell Banker Residential Brokerage offices in Back Bay, Boston, MA for more than two decades. He oversees 85 agents in the selling and renting of condominiums, townhouses and cooperatives in the luxury market. His specialty is working with developers in the areas of historic renovation and mid-rise new construction.

Ken is recognized by the agents and staff he manages for his approachable, yet direct, style, and for his kindness and caring. As some of his agents have said, *"He has always been there for me." "He's perceptive and intuitive; he's not just a manager, he's an advisor and coach." "He's been the most important mentor I have ever had throughout my entire sales career."*

Ken's motto is, *"Giving back is in my DNA, and nurturing Boston is an honor."* He is active on many local boards, including Community Servings and the Back Bay Association. Ken was recently appointed as a city commissioner on the Back Bay Architectural Commission.

Ken is a classically trained musician and a former museum curator. He lives in Boston's South End.

**"If we did all the things we are capable of,
we would literally astound ourselves."**
– Thomas A. Edison

A portion of the proceeds from sales of this book is being donated to the National Forest Foundation to support reforestation projects in the U.S.

Made in the USA
Middletown, DE
19 June 2018